5 Ingredients Instant Pot Cookbook

1500 Easy Recipes to Get Meals Faster for Busy People to Master Your Instant Pot and Spend Less Kitchen Time with 5 Ingredients

Georgina Flynn

CONTENTS

BEEF & LAMB , PORK RECIPES 59

VEGETABLE & VEGETARIAN RECIPES.................72

PASTA & RICE RECIPES.................85

SOUPS, STEWS & CHILIS RECIPES 93

SNACKS & DESSERTS , APPETIZERS RECIPES 99

APPENDIX : RECIPES INDEX 115

INTRODUCTION

I am a mother of two kids. One day last month, I go back home and find my children in their pajamas sitting on the couch watching TV and enjoying snacks. As I pass by the kitchen, I notice that there are groceries all over the counter, a milk spilled on the floor, and water all over the place from when kids were playing in it. Dinner is running late. They excitedly ran up to me telling me about their day but I yelled at them for making a mess and failing to take care of themselves. I scream at them for not completing their homework, taking shower, or getting dinner ready. I already feel anxious about arguing with them about not finishing their work. They questioned why I'm yelling at them when they are so pleased to have me home, I stop and ask if they would prefer to help prepare supper and cook instead of watching TV. They agree and we work together to prepare a delicious meal. They are proud of themselves. While I finish my book, they tidy up the kitchen, put the groceries away, and finish their homework.

See, preparing dinner together with your family has a magic, which can wipe the stress out and eliminate worries. In our kitchen time, they share what happened in school and I share what happen in my work. We prepare ingredients, cook meals and share everything together. Sometimes, yelling could not deal with anything, but spending time with families could solve lots of problems.

Especially if you have an instant pot, it will helps more for quick, easy and efficient meal, combining with 5 ingredients, and more recipes. I can make a whole chicken in 15 minutes instead of an hour, and everything is cooked much more evenly. You'll be amazing about how the meals done all in one pot. It'll be the best investment you make.

This cookbook shows you how to use your instant pot, and how to make mouth-watering meals for your families. With a few accessories and this right recipes, your multi-cooker can get cozy soups, crowd-pleasing chicken dinners, healthy weeknight meals and even desserts on the table with ease. Ready to put your Instant Pot to good use? You're in the right place — we've got plenty of delicious options for you to choose from.

Get to Know Instant Pot

The primary cooking function on every Instant Pot is pressure cooking. You can customize the pressure level and cooking time depending on what you're cooking, or press buttons with cooking settings specific to certain foods, like rice, bean, poultry, multigrain and more.

Instant Pot models differ in terms of the cooking functions each offers beyond pressure cooking — certain models offer functions like sauté, yogurt, sous vide, slow cooker and more.

The core of an Instant Pot is an electric pressure cooker. It uses hot steam and pressure to cook food. Food is being boiled at a high pressure, so it's not going to satisfy you if you only like crunchy food. Notice that dishes that come out of the Instant Pot often have a moist rather than crispy texture.

However, Instant Pots are different from traditional electric pressure cookers. All of Instant Pots' different pressure settings are slightly higher than that of a traditional pressure cooker, this helps it cook meals faster than a standard electric pressure cooker. With versatile usage of Instant Pot, home chefs of all skill levels can use them to make a variety of dishes. Another benefit of the Instant Pot is that it can help you make meals at a lower cost. The Instant Pot does a really good job of taking some ingredients that are not expensive and turning them into something delicious.

How do Instant Pots work?

Cooking food in the Instant Pot is not instantaneous — as the appliance's name might suggest — although it does speed up the process overall. Instant Pots need time to heat up so their temperature can rise above boiling point, which is 212 degrees Fahrenheit at sea level. As it heats up, food inside the Instant Pot releases steam, and the device traps the steam inside. The build-up of steam inside the Instant Pot creates a high-pressure environment — when the device reaches an optimal pressure point, a pressure valve lifts into place and steam is released through a vent on the appliance's lid. That's when the food's cooking time begins.

You should get a pretty clear idea of different parts of the Instant Pot from the provided manual but in short, any Instant Pot model has three main components:

-- Cooker Base pot with a heating element on the inside and a control panel on the front. This part doesn't go in the dishwasher.

-- Inner Pot is where the food goes in. It's made from stainless steel and comes out; it can be cleaned by hand or in a dishwasher.

-- The lid – which has a sealing ring on the inside that keeps all the pressure and steam in the pot, as well as the key features on top that you will use on regular basis.

In short, the temperature and pressure inside an Instant Pot pressure cooker are constantly monitored and adjusted by a smart microprocessor. The same element takes commands from the control panel and turns them into instructions for the heating element.

However, no IP will start cooking if the lid is not closed, the sealing ring is not in tip-top shape, or the steam release valve is not in the right position. So, it's a teamwork effort between several elements that make possible this technical marvel exists in your kitchen.

Are Instant Pots safe?

One of the main reasons people are often hesitate about purchasing an Instant Pot — or an electric pressure cooker in general — is safety. Stovetop pressure cookers got a bad reputation because their lids were relatively easy to remove before the pressure was released, which ran the risk of burns and messes, experts told us. But electric pressure cookers like the Instant Pot are incredibly safe compared to stovetop pressure cookers."

Instant Pots are designed with safety mechanisms so they'll shut down if something goes wrong. One of those safety mechanisms is a burn notice that's triggered if the Instant Pot overheats and food begins to burn — the device shuts off completely in this case.

It's crucial to read your Instant Pot's instruction manual before you use the appliance. Make sure you know what all the buttons mean before you use the appliance. It's also important to consider the place you put the appliance in your kitchen while using it: Since steam comes out the top, you need to place the Instant Pot in an area where there's a lot of open space above and around the appliance for that steam to ventilate into. And make sure you never cover the vent on your Instant Pot — the steam needs to escape in order for the pressure to lower inside the Instant Pot, allowing you to remove the lid when your food is done cooking.

Safety tips

There are plenty of safety precautions you need to take when using the pressure cooking program. Follow these safety tips and you'll make yourself proud.

Keep away from the steam

This is a tip that stayed true for old pressure cooker through to the modern digital versions. Don't put any exposed body part over the steam valve unless you want a nasty burn. Also be sure to keep your Instant Pot out of the reach of children.

Be careful with the lid

A lid that's off kilter or unlocked can explode off and cause burns. It is important to lock the lid properly before any pressure cooking. Always double-check that the sealing ring is properly in position under the lid, clean and free of debris before cooking. Otherwise, your lid may not seal. Finally, twist the lid clockwise and align the arrow with the locked icon to get the pot to lock properly. Your display should flash "Lid" if it isn't placed correctly.

Fill your cooker the right way

Too much food or liquid in your Instant Pot while pressure cooking can lead to dangerous pressure levels. Don't let the total amount of precooked food and liquid in the inner pot go over the two-thirds line. If you are pressure cooking food that expands like rice, beans, pasta or dried vegetables, be even more careful.

Leave the Instant Pot do its job

Using with an Instant Pot is easier because it can time everything for you, so let it do its job. The pressure cooker can take from a few minutes at the very least to 40 or more to get to where it needs to be. Do not open the cooker until it has depressurized completely to avoid explosions, even if you just want a quick peek.

Measurement Conversions

BASIC KITCHEN CONVERSIONS & EQUIVALENTS

DRY MEASUREMENTS CONVERSION CHART

3 TEASPOONS = 1 TABLESPOON = 1/16 CUP

6 TEASPOONS = 2 TABLESPOONS = 1/8 CUP

12 TEASPOONS = 4 TABLESPOONS = 1/4 CUP

24 TEASPOONS = 8 TABLESPOONS = 1/2 CUP

36 TEASPOONS = 12 TABLESPOONS = 3/4 CUP

48 TEASPOONS = 16 TABLESPOONS = 1 CUP

METRIC TO US COOKING CONVERSIONS

OVEN TEMPERATURES

120 °C = 250 °F

160 °C = 320 °F

180° C = 350 °F

205 °C = 400 °F

220 °C = 425 °F

LIQUID MEASUREMENTS CONVERSION CHART

8 FLUID OUNCES = 1 CUP = 1/2 PINT = 1/4 QUART

16 FLUID OUNCES = 2 CUPS = 1 PINT = 1/2 QUART

32 FLUID OUNCES = 4 CUPS = 2 PINTS = 1 QUART = 1/4 GALLON

128 FLUID OUNCES = 16 CUPS = 8 PINTS = 4 QUARTS = 1 GALLON

BAKING IN GRAMS

1 CUP FLOUR = 140 GRAMS

1 CUP SUGAR = 150 GRAMS

1 CUP POWDERED SUGAR = 160 GRAMS

1 CUP HEAVY CREAM = 235 GRAMS

VOLUME

1 MILLILITER = 1/5 TEASPOON

5 ML = 1 TEASPOON

15 ML = 1 TABLESPOON

240 ML = 1 CUP OR 8 FLUID OUNCES

1 LITER = 34 FL. OUNCES

WEIGHT

1 GRAM = .035 OUNCES

100 GRAMS = 3.5 OUNCES

500 GRAMS = 1.1 POUNDS

1 KILOGRAM = 35 OUNCES

US TO METRIC COOKING CONVERSIONS

1/5 TSP = 1 ML

1 TSP = 5 ML

1 TBSP = 15 ML

1 FL OUNCE = 30 ML

1 CUP = 237 ML

1 PINT (2 CUPS) = 473 ML

1 QUART (4 CUPS) = .95 LITER

1 GALLON (16 CUPS) = 3.8 LITERS

1 OZ = 28 GRAMS

1 POUND = 454 GRAMS

BUTTER

1 CUP BUTTER = 2 STICKS = 8 OUNCES = 230 GRAMS = 8 TABLESPOONS

WHAT DOES 1 CUP EQUAL

1 CUP = 8 FLUID OUNCES

1 CUP = 16 TABLESPOONS

1 CUP = 48 TEASPOONS

1 CUP = 1/2 PINT

1 CUP = 1/4 QUART

1 CUP = 1/16 GALLON

1 CUP = 240 ML

BAKING PAN CONVERSIONS

1 CUP ALL-PURPOSE FLOUR = 4.5 OZ

1 CUP ROLLED OATS = 3 OZ 1 LARGE EGG = 1.7 OZ

1 CUP BUTTER = 8 OZ 1 CUP MILK = 8 OZ

1 CUP HEAVY CREAM = 8.4 OZ

1 CUP GRANULATED SUGAR = 7.1 OZ

1 CUP PACKED BROWN SUGAR = 7.75 OZ

1 CUP VEGETABLE OIL = 7.7 OZ

1 CUP UNSIFTED POWDERED SUGAR = 4.4 OZ

BAKING PAN CONVERSIONS

9-INCH ROUND CAKE PAN = 12 CUPS

10-INCH TUBE PAN =16 CUPS

11-INCH BUNDT PAN = 12 CUPS

9-INCH SPRINGFORM PAN = 10 CUPS

9 X 5 INCH LOAF PAN = 8 CUPS

9-INCH SQUARE PAN = 8 CUPS

Breakfast Recipes

Breakfast Recipes

Cranberry Beans Salad

Serves:4 | Cooking Time: 15 Mins

Ingredients:

- 3 tbsps. olive oil
- 1 ½ cups fresh green beans
- 5 tbsps. apple cider vinegar
- ½ red onion, chopped
- 1 cup cranberry beans, soaked and drained
- 1 cup water

Directions:

1. Add 1 cup water and steamer basket to your Instant Pot.
2. Place the cranberry beans and green beans in the basket.
3. Lock the lid. Select the Manual mode and cook for 15 minutes at High Pressure.
4. Once cooking is complete, do a quick pressure release. Carefully open the lid.
5. Drain all beans and transfer them to a salad bowl. Add the onions, vinegar, and olive oil, and gently toss to combine. Serve immediately.

Breakfast Burritos

Serves:2 | Cooking Time: 25 Minutes

Ingredients:

- Nonstick Cooking Spray
- 4 Large Eggs
- ¼ Cup Shredded Cheddar Cheese
- ¼ Teaspoon Salt
- ⅛ Teaspoon Black Pepper
- ¾ Cup Frozen Potatoes O'Brien (With Onions And Peppers)
- ⅓ Cup Chopped Ham
- 2 Burrito-Size Flour Tortillas

Directions:

1. Spray a 6- Or 7-Inch Round Pan (Whatever Fits Best In Your Instant Pot) With Cooking Spray.
2. In a Small Bowl, Whisk Together The Eggs, Cheese, Salt, And Pepper.
3. Scatter The Frozen Potatoes In The Bottom Of The Prepared Pan. Top With The Ham.
4. Pour The Egg Mixture On Top. Cover The Pan Tightly With Aluminum Foil.
5. Place a Trivet In The Bottom Of The Instant Pot, Then Pour In 1½ Cups Water. Place The Pan On The Trivet.
6. Lock The Lid In Place. Select Pressure Cook And Adjust The Pressure To High And The Time To 25 Minutes. After Cooking, Let The Pressure Release Naturally For 5 Minutes, Then Quick Release Any Remaining Pressure.
7. Once The Float Valve Drops, Open The Lid And Carefully Remove The Pan From The Instant Pot.
8. Stir To Combine, Then Spoon Into Tortillas, Roll Up, And Serve Warm.

Cheesy Bacon Quiche

Serves:6 | Cooking Time: 10 Mins

Ingredients:

- 2 tbsps. olive oil
- 6 eggs, lightly beaten
- 1 cup milk
- Salt and pepper, to taste
- 2 cups Monterey Jack cheese, grated
- 1 cup bacon, cooked and crumbled

Directions:

1. Grease the Instant Pot with olive oil.
2. Combine the eggs, milk, salt, and pepper in a large bowl. Stir to mix well.
3. Put the cheese and bacon in the pot, then pour the egg mixture over. Stir to mix well.
4. Lock the lid. Set to Manual mode, then set the timer for 10 minutes at High Pressure.
5. Once the timer goes off, perform a natural pressure release for 5 minutes. Carefully open the lid.
6. Transfer the quiche on a plate and serve.

Blueberry Breakfast Bowl

Serves:4 | Cooking Time: 10 Mins

Ingredients:

- 1 cup apple juice
- 3 tbsps. blueberries
- 1½ cups water
- 1 tbsp. honey
- 1½ cups quinoa

Directions:

1. In the Instant Pot, stir together the water with quinoa.
2. Lock the lid. Select the Manual mode and set the cooking time for 2 minutes at High Pressure.
3. Once cooking is complete, do a natural pressure release for 10 minutes, then release any remaining pressure. Carefully open the lid.
4. Divide the quinoa into four bowls. Drizzle each bowl evenly with honey and apple juice. Sprinkle the blueberries on top and serve.

Monkey Bread

Serves:2 | Cooking Time: 20 Minutes

Ingredients:

- Nonstick Cooking Spray
- 3 Tablespoons Granulated Sugar
- ¼ Teaspoon Ground Cinnamon
- 1 (7.5-Ounce) Container Canned Biscuits
- 2 Tablespoons Butter, Melted
- ¼ Cup Packed Light Brown Sugar

Directions:

1. Spray a 3-Cup Bundt Pan (Or Other Nonstick Round Pan) With Cooking Spray.
2. In a Small Bowl, Mix The Granulated Sugar And Cinnamon Together.
3. Open The Can Of Biscuits And Cut Each Biscuit Into Four Pieces.
4. Dunk Each Piece Into The Cinnamon-Sugar Mixture And Roll To Coat. Place In The Prepared Pan.
5. In a Small Bowl, Stir Together The Melted Butter And Brown Sugar. Drizzle The Mixture Over The Biscuit Pieces. Cover The Pan Tightly With Aluminum Foil.
6. Place a Trivet In The Bottom Of The Instant Pot, Then Pour In 1½ Cups Water. Place The Pan On The Trivet.
7. Lock The Lid In Place. Select Pressure Cook And

Adjust The Pressure To High And The Time To 20 Minutes. After Cooking, Move The Steam Release Handle To Venting And Quick Release The Pressure.
8. Once The Float Valve Drops, Open The Lid And Carefully Remove The Pan From The Instant Pot.
9. Let The Pan Sit For 10 Minutes, Then Invert Onto a Plate. Serve Warm.
10. Per Serving: Calories: 607; Carbohydrates: 95g; Fat: 23g; Fiber: 1g; Protein: 7g; Sugar: 53g; Sodium: 839mg

Eggs And Bacon Breakfast Risotto

Serves:2 | Cooking Time: 12 Mins

Ingredients:

- 1½ cups chicken stock
- 2 poached eggs
- 2 tbsps. grated Parmesan cheese
- 3 chopped bacon slices
- ¾ cup Arborio rice

Directions:

1. Set your Instant Pot to Sauté and add the bacon and cook for 5 minutes until crispy, stirring occasionally.
2. Carefully stir in the rice and let cook for an additional 1 minute.
3. Add the chicken stock and stir well.
4. Lock the lid. Select the Manual mode and set the cooking time for 6 minutes at Low Pressure.
5. Once cooking is complete, do a quick pressure release. Carefully open the lid.
6. Add the Parmesan cheese and keep stirring until melted. Divide the risotto between two plates. Add the eggs on the side and serve immediately.

French Toast Casserole

Serves:2 | Cooking Time: 25 Minutes

Ingredients:

- Nonstick Cooking Spray
- 1 Large Egg
- 1 Cup Milk
- ¼ Cup Plus 1 Tablespoon Packed Light Brown Sugar, Divided
- ½ Teaspoon Ground Cinnamon
- 3 Cups Sourdough Bread Cubes
- Maple Syrup, For Topping (Optional)

Directions:

1. Spray a 6- Or 7-Inch Round Pan (Whatever Fits

Best In Your Instant Pot) With Cooking Spray.

2. In a Small Bowl, Whisk Together The Egg, Milk, ¼ Cup Of Brown Sugar, And Cinnamon.

3. Scatter The Bread Cubes In The Prepared Pan And Cover With The Egg Mixture. Let This Set For 5 Minutes To Allow The Bread To Soak Up The Egg Mixture.

4. Sprinkle The Remaining 1 Tablespoon Of Brown Sugar On Top Of The Bread. Cover The Pan Tightly With Aluminum Foil.

5. Place a Trivet In The Bottom Of The Instant Pot, Then Pour In 1½ Cups Water. Place The Pan On The Trivet.

6. Lock The Lid In Place. Select Pressure Cook And Adjust The Pressure To High And The Time To 25 Minutes. After Cooking, Let The Pressure Release Naturally For 5 Minutes, Then Quick Release Any Remaining Pressure.

7. Once The Float Valve Drops, Open The Lid And Carefully Remove The Pan From The Instant Pot.

8. Serve Warm With Maple Syrup, If You Like.

Breakfast Cobbler

Serves:2 | Cooking Time: 15 Mins

Ingredients:

- 2 tbsps. honey
- ¼ cup shredded coconut
- 1 plum, pitted and chopped
- 3 tbsps. coconut oil, divided
- 1 apple, cored and chopped

Directions:

1. In the Instant Pot, combine the plum with apple, half of the coconut oil, and honey, and blend well.

2. Lock the lid. Select the Manual mode and cook for 10 minutes at High Pressure.

3. Once cooking is complete, do a quick pressure release. Carefully open the lid.

4. Transfer the mixture to bowls and clean your Instant Pot.

5. Set your Instant Pot to Sauté and heat the remaining coconut oil. Add the coconut, stir, and toast for 5 minutes.

6. Sprinkle the coconut over fruit mixture and serve.

Spanish Tortilla With Red Bell Pepper Sauce

Serves:4 | Cooking Time: 15 Minutes

Ingredients:

- 2 tablespoons olive oil
- ½ medium yellow onion, thinly sliced
- 1 large (12-ounce) russet potato, peeled and cut into 1/16-inch slices, or 1½ cups hash browns such as Simply Potatoes brand
- Salt and freshly ground black pepper
- 8 large eggs
- ½ teaspoon smoked paprika
- 1 cup drained jarred roasted red peppers

Directions:

1. Spray a 7 × 3-inch round metal baking pan with cooking spray and line the bottom with a round of parchment paper; spray the parchment, too.

2. Put the oil in the pot, select SAUTÉ, and adjust to NORMAL/MEDIUM heat. When the oil is hot, add the onion and cook, stirring frequently, until beginning to soften, 3 minutes. Add the potato, 1 teaspoon salt, and several grinds of pepper and stir to combine. Cover loosely with the lid set to "Venting" and cook, stirring frequently, until the potatoes are barely tender when pierced with a fork, 4 to 5 minutes. Press CANCEL.

3. Scrape the onion and potato into the prepared pan. In a small bowl, whisk together the eggs with ¼ teaspoon of the paprika. Pour the egg mixture into the baking pan over the potato mixture.

4. Pour 1½ cups water into the pot and set a trivet with handles in the pot. Place the baking pan, uncovered, on the trivet. Lock on the lid, select the PRESSURE COOK function, and adjust to HIGH pressure for 10 minutes. Make sure the steam valve is in the "Sealing" position.

5. 5 While the tortilla is cooking, blend the roasted peppers with the remaining ¼ teaspoon smoked paprika and a few grinds of pepper until smooth. Set aside.

6. When the cooking time is up, let the pressure come down naturally for 10 minutes and then quick-release the remaining pressure. Carefully remove the pan from the pot. Run a knife around the edges of the pan, place a dinner plate over the pan, and carefully invert the tortilla onto the plate. Discard the parchment paper. Cut the tortilla into wedges and serve with the sauce.

Mini Frittata

Serves:6 | Cooking Time: 12 Mins

Ingredients:

- 1 chopped red bell pepper
- 1 tbsp. almond milk
- ¼ tsp. salt
- 2 tbsps. grated Cheddar cheese
- 5 whisked eggs
- 1½ cups water

Directions:

1. In a bowl, combine the salt, eggs, cheese, almond milk, and red bell pepper, and whisk well. Pour the egg mixture into 6 baking molds.
2. Add 1½ cups water and steamer basket to your Instant Pot. Transfer the baking molds to the basket.
3. Lock the lid. Select the Manual mode and cook for 5minutes at High Pressure.
4. Once cooking is complete, do a quick pressure release. Carefully open the lid. Serve hot.

Breakfast Arugula Salad

Serves:6 | Cooking Time: 15 Mins

Ingredients:

- 2 blood oranges, peeled and sliced
- 2 cups water
- 4 oz. arugula
- 1 tsp. sunflower oil
- 1 cup kamut grains, soaked

Directions:

1. In the Instant Pot, combine the kamut grains with sunflower oil and water, and whisk well.
2. Lock the lid. Select the Manual mode and set the cooking time for 15 minutes at High Pressure.
3. Once cooking is complete, do a natural pressure release for 10 minutes, then release any remaining pressure. Carefully open the lid.
4. Drain the kamut grains and transfer to a large bowl. Add the arugula and oranges, and toss well. Serve immediately.

Celeriac And Bacon Mix

Serves:6 | Cooking Time: 10 Mins

Ingredients:

- 2 tbsps. chicken stock
- 2 tsps. dried parsley
- 4 oz. shredded Cheddar cheese
- 3 bacon strips
- 2 lbs. peeled and cubed celeriac

Directions:

1. Set the Instant Pot to Sauté and cook the bacon for 2 minutes.
2. Add the parsley, celeriac and stock, and stir.
3. Lock the lid. Select the Manual mode and cook for 6 minutes at High Pressure.
4. Once cooking is complete, do a quick pressure release. Carefully open the lid.
5. Add the cheese and keep stirring until melted. Serve warm.

Turkey Breast And Avocado Breakfast

Serves:4 | Cooking Time: 7 Mins

Ingredients:

- 4 whisked eggs
- 4 avocado slices
- 2 tbsps. olive oil
- 2 tbsps. vegetable stock
- 4 cooked turkey breast slices

Directions:

1. Set the Instant Pot to Sauté and heat the olive oil.
2. Add the turkey and brown for 2 minutes, then transfer to a plate.
3. Add the eggs and vegetable stock to the pot and whisk well.
4. Lock the lid. Select the Manual mode and cook for 5 minutes at High Pressure.
5. Once cooking is complete, do a quick pressure release. Carefully open the lid.
6. Divide the eggs and avocado slices next to turkey breast slices and serve

Pomegranate Porridge

Serves:4 | Cooking Time: 6 Mins

Ingredients:

- 2 pomegranates seeds
- 2 tbsps. sugar
- 2 cups shredded coconut
- 1 cup pomegranate juice
- 2 cup water

Directions:

1. In the Instant Pot, combine the coconut with water and pomegranate juice, and whisk well.
2. Lock the lid. Select the Manual mode and cook for 3 minutes at High Pressure.
3. Once cooking is complete, do a natural pressure release for 5 minutes, then release any remaining pressure. Carefully open the lid.
4. Add the pomegranate seeds and sugar and give a good stir. Ladle into bowls and serve warm.

Apple Cinnamon Oatmeal

Serves:4 | Cooking Time: 8 Mins

Ingredients:

- 1 tsp. cinnamon powder
- 1 chopped apple
- 1 cup steel-cut oats
- ¼ tsp. ground nutmeg
- 3 cups water
- Salt, to taste

Directions:

1. Add all the ingredients to your Instant Pot and stir to combine.
2. Lock the lid. Select the Manual mode and set the cooking time for 8 minutes at High Pressure.
3. Once cooking is complete, do a natural pressure release for 5 minutes. Carefully open the lid.
4. Divide the oatmeal among four serving bowls and serve warm.

Speedy Soft-boiled Eggs

Serves:4 | Cooking Time: 10 Minutes

Ingredients:

- 4 large eggs
- Salt and pepper to taste

Directions:

1. To the pressure cooker, add 1 cup of water and place a wire rack. Place eggs on it. Seal the lid, press Steam, and cook for 3 minutes on High Pressure. Do a quick release.
2. Allow to cool in an ice bath. Peel the eggs and season with salt and pepper before serving.

Pearl Barley Porridge

Serves:6 | Cooking Time: 12 Mins

Ingredients:

- 3 tbsps. lemon juice
- 1 red bell pepper, chopped
- 1 onion, sliced
- 1 cup pearl barley
- 3 cups vegetable stock

Directions:

1. Add the barley and stock to the Instant Pot and stir well.
2. Press the Manual button and set the cooking time for 12 minutes at High Pressure.
3. Once cooking is complete, do a natural pressure release for 6 minutes. Carefully open the lid.
4. Transfer to a bowl and stir in the remaining ingredients, then serve.

Greek Yogurt With Honey & Walnuts

Serves:10 | Cooking Time: 15hr

Ingredients:

- 2 tbsp Greek yogurt
- 8 cups milk
- ¼ cup sugar honey
- 1 tsp vanilla extract
- 1 cup walnuts, chopped

Directions:

1. Add the milk to your Instant Pot. Seal the lid and press Yogurt until the display shows "Boil". When the cooking cycle is over, the display will show Yogurt.

Open the lid and check that milk temperature is at least 175°F. Get rid of the skin lying on the milk's surface. Let cool in an ice bath until it becomes warm to the touch.

2. In a bowl, mix one cup of milk and yogurt to make a smooth consistency. Mix the milk with yogurt mixture. Transfer to the pot and place on your Pressure cooker.

3. Seal the lid, press Yogurt, and adjust the timer to 9 hrs. Once cooking is complete, strain the yogurt into a bowl using a strainer with cheesecloth. Chill for 4 hours.

4. Add in vanilla and honey and gently stir well. Spoon the yogurt into glass jars. Serve sprinkled with walnuts and enjoy

Sausage And Egg Casserole

Serves:2 | Cooking Time: 20 Minutes

Ingredients:

- Nonstick Cooking Spray
- 1 Tablespoon Olive Oil
- 8 Ounces Loose Breakfast Sausage
- 4 Large Eggs
- ¼ Cup Milk
- ½ Cup Shredded Cheddar Cheese
- ½ Teaspoon Salt
- ¼ Teaspoon Black Pepper

Directions:

1. Spray a 6- Or 7-Inch Round Pan (Whatever Fits Best In Your Instant Pot) With Cooking Spray.

2. Set The Instant Pot To Sauté And Pour In The Olive Oil.

3. Once The Oil Is Shimmering, Add The Breakfast Sausage. Cook The Sausage, Stirring To Break Up The Meat, Until Cooked Through, 4 To 5 Minutes. Once Cooked, Press Cancel To Turn Off The Instant Pot.

4. Transfer The Sausage To a Plate And Wipe Out The Inner Pot With Paper Towels.

5. In a Small Bowl, Whisk Together The Eggs, Milk, Cheese, Salt, And Pepper.

6. Scatter The Frozen Potatoes In The Bottom Of The Prepared Pan. Top With The Sausage.

7. Pour The Egg Mixture On Top Of The Potatoes And Sausage. Cover The Pan Tightly With Aluminum Foil.

8. Place a Trivet In The Bottom Of The Instant Pot, Then Pour In 1½ Cups Water. Place The Pan On The Trivet.

9. Lock The Lid In Place. Select Pressure Cook And Adjust The Pressure To High And The Time To 15 Minutes. After Cooking, Let The Pressure Release Naturally For 5 Minutes, Then Quick Release Any Remaining Pressure.

10. Once The Float Valve Drops, Open The Lid And Carefully Remove The Pan From The Instant Pot.

11. Slice The Casserole Into 4 Pieces And Serve Warm.

Potato And Spinach Hash

Serves:4 | Cooking Time: 10 Mins

Ingredients:

- ¼ tsp. salt
- 1 small yellow onion, chopped
- 3 baked sweet potatoes, peeled and cubed
- 11 oz. baby spinach
- 12 oz. chopped chorizo

Directions:

1. Set the Instant Pot to Sauté and add the chorizo and onion. Cook for 2 to 3 minutes.

2. Add the potato cubes, baby spinach and salt, and stir to combine.

3. Lock the lid. Select the Manual mode and cook for 7 minutes at High Pressure.

4. Once cooking is complete, do a quick pressure release. Carefully open the lid.

5. Divide the mixture between plates and serve.

Special Pancake

Serves:4 | Cooking Time: 30 Mins

Ingredients:

- 2½ tsps. baking powder
- 2 eggs, beaten
- 2 tbsps. sugar
- 1½ cups milk
- 2 cups white flour

Directions:

1. In a bowl, mix the flour with eggs, milk, sugar, and baking powder. Stir to incorporate.

2. Spread out the mixture onto the bottom of the Instant Pot.

3. Lock the lid. Select the Manual mode and cook for 30 minutes at High Pressure.

4. Once cooking is complete, do a quick pressure release. Carefully open the lid.

5. Let the pancake cool for a few minutes before slicing to serve

Veggie Quiche

Serves:6 | Cooking Time: 20 Mins

Ingredients:

- ½ cup milk
- 1 red bell pepper, chopped
- 2 green onions, chopped
- Salt, to taste
- 8 whisked eggs
- 1 cup water

Directions:

1. In a bowl, combine the whisked eggs with milk, bell pepper, onions and salt, and stir well. Pour the egg mixture into a pan.
2. In your Instant Pot, add the water and trivet. Place the pan on the trivet and cover with tin foil.
3. Lock the lid. Select the Manual mode and cook for 20 minutes at High Pressure.
4. Once cooking is complete, do a quick pressure release. Carefully open the lid.
5. Slice the quiche and divide between plates to serve.

Hard-"boiled" Eggs

Serves:6 | Cooking Time: 6 Minutes

Ingredients:

- 1 cup water
- 6 large eggs

Directions:

1. Add water to the Instant Pot and insert steamer basket. Place eggs in basket. Lock lid.
2. Press the Manual or Pressure Cook button and adjust time to 6 minutes. When timer beeps, quick-release pressure until float valve drops. Unlock lid.
3. Create an ice bath by adding 1 cup ice and 1 cup water to a medium bowl. Transfer eggs to ice bath to stop the cooking process.
4. Peel eggs. Slice each egg directly onto a plate. Serve immediately.

Pumpkin Spice Oatmeal

Serves:2 | Cooking Time: 10 Mins

Ingredients:

- ¼ tsp. ground cinnamon
- ⅛ tsp. ground pumpkin spice
- 1 cup steel-cut oats
- 1 tbsp. sugar
- 1 cup almond milk
- 1½ cups water

Directions:

1. Place all ingredients into your Instant Pot and mix well.
2. Lock the lid. Select the Manual mode and set the cooking time for 6 minutes at High Pressure.
3. Once cooking is complete, do a natural pressure release for 5 minutes. Carefully open the lid.
4. Ladle into two serving bowls and serve.

Bread Pudding

Serves:8 | Cooking Time: 15 Mins

Ingredients:

- ½ cup maple syrup
- 1 bread loaf, cubed
- ½ cup butter
- 2 cups coconut milk
- 4 eggs
- 2 cups water

Directions:

1. In a blender, blend the coconut milk with eggs, butter and maple syrup until smooth.
2. Transfer the mixture to a pudding pan and add the bread cubes. Cover the pan with tin foil.
3. Add 2 cups water and trivet to your Instant Pot. Place the pudding pan on the trivet.
4. Lock the lid. Select the Manual mode and cook for15 minutes at High Pressure.
5. Once cooking is complete, do a quick pressure release. Carefully open the lid.
6. Allow to cool for 5 minutes before serving.

Cauliflower Breakfast Hash

Serves:4 | Cooking Time: 7 Mins

Ingredients:

- 4 eggs
- 4 chopped jalapeño peppers
- 1 tbsp. olive oil
- 3 minced garlic cloves
- 1 grated cauliflower head, liquid squeezed out
- Salt and pepper, to taste
- ½ cup water

Directions:

1. Press the Sauté button on the Instant Pot and heat the oil.
2. Stir in the garlic and sauté for 1 minute until fragrant.
3. Stir in the grated cauliflower, pepper and salt.
4. Pour in ½ cup water and spread the cauliflower mixture evenly in the bottom of the Instant Pot.
5. Make four wells in the cauliflower and gently crack an egg into each well.
6. Sprinkle with jalapeño peppers.
7. Lock the lid. Select the Manual mode and set the cooking time for 6 minutes at High Pressure.
8. Once cooking is complete, do a quick pressure release. Carefully open the lid.
9. Cool for a few minutes and serve on plates.

Steel-cut Oatmeal

Serves:2 | Cooking Time: 17 Minutes

Ingredients:

- Nonstick Cooking Spray
- 1 Cup Steel-Cut Oats
- 1½ Cups Water
- 1 Cup Nondairy Milk (Such As Almond Or Oat Milk)
- ⅛ Teaspoon Salt
- Brown Sugar, Chopped Fresh Fruit, And/Or Nuts, For Topping (Optional)

Directions:

1. Spray The Bottom Of The Instant Pot With Cooking Spray.
2. Add The Oats, Water, Nondairy Milk, And Salt And Stir To Combine.
3. Lock The Lid In Place. Select Pressure Cook And Adjust The Pressure To High And The Time To 2 Minutes. After Cooking, Let The Pressure Release Naturally For 5 Minutes, Then Quick Release Any Remaining Pressure.
4. Once The Float Valve Drops, Open The Lid And Stir The Oatmeal.
5. Serve Warm With Your Favorite Toppings.

Broccoli And Egg Casserole

Serves:6 | Cooking Time: 15 Mins

Ingredients:

- 6 eggs, beaten
- ⅓ cup all-purpose flour
- 3 cups cottage cheese
- ¼ cup butter, melted
- Salt and pepper, to taste
- 2 tbsps. chopped onions
- 3 cups broccoli florets

Directions:

1. Combine the eggs, flour, cheese, butter, salt, and pepper in a large bowl. Stir to mix well.
2. Put the onions and broccoli in the Instant Pot. Pour the egg mixture over. Stir to combine well.
3. Lock the lid. Set to Manual mode, then set the timer to 15 minutes at High pressure.
4. Once the timer goes off, perform a natural pressure release for 10 minutes, then release any remaining pressure. Carefully open the lid.
5. Transfer them on a plate and serve immediately

French Eggs

Serves:4 | Cooking Time: 8 Mins

Ingredients:

- ¼ tsp. salt
- 4 bacon slices
- 1 tbsp. olive oil
- 4 tbsps. chopped chives
- 4 eggs
- 1½ cups water

Directions:

1. Grease 4 ramekins with a drizzle of oil and crack an egg into each ramekin.
2. Add a bacon slice on top and season with salt. Sprinkle the chives on top.
3. Add 1½ cups water and steamer basket to your Instant Pot. Transfer the ramekins to the basket.
4. Lock the lid. Select the Manual mode and set the cooking time for 8 minutes at High Pressure.

5. Once cooking is complete, do a quick pressure release. Carefully open the lid.
6. Serve your baked eggs immediately.

Breakfast Coconut Yogurt

Serves:4 | Cooking Time: 8 Hours

Ingredients:

- 2 cans coconut cream
- 1 package yogurt starter
- 1 tbsp. gelatin

Directions:

1. Pour the coconut cream into the Instant Pot.
2. Lock the lid. Select the Yogurt mode, then bring to a boil at High Pressure.
3. When the coconut cream boils, perform a natural pressure release. Carefully open the lid.
4. Add the yogurt starter and stir to mix well.
5. Lock the lid. Set the timer for 8 hours to ferment at High Pressure.
6. When the timer goes off, perform a normal release for 10 minutes, then release any remaining pressure. Carefully open the lid.
7. Stir in the gelatin and keep stirring until smooth.
8. Pour the yogurt in a jar or a glass and put in the refrigerator for at least 6 hours before serving.

Swiss Chard Salad

Serves:4 | Cooking Time: 12 Mins

Ingredients:

- ¼ tsp. red pepper flakes
- 1 bunch Swiss chard, sliced
- ¼ cup toasted pine nuts
- 1 tbsp. balsamic vinegar
- 2 tbsps. olive oil

Directions:

1. Set your Instant Pot to Sauté and heat the olive oil.
2. Add the chard, stir, and cook for 2 minutes until tender.
3. Add pepper flakes and vinegar and stir well.
4. Lock the lid. Select the Steam mode and cook for 3 minutes at High Pressure.
5. Sprinkle with the pine nuts and divide into bowls to serve.

Cheesy Egg And Bacon Muffins

Serves:4 | Cooking Time: 8 Mins

Ingredients:

- 4 cooked bacon slices, crumbled
- 4 tbsps. shredded Cheddar cheese
- ¼ tsp. salt
- 1 green onion, chopped
- 4 eggs, beaten
- 1½ cups water

Directions:

1. In a bowl, mix the eggs with cheese, bacon, onion and salt, and whisk well. Pour the egg mixture evenly into four muffin cups.
2. Add 1½ cups water and steamer basket to the Instant Pot. Place the muffin cups in the basket.
3. Lock the lid. Select the Manual mode and set the cooking time for 8 minutes at High Pressure.
4. Once cooking is complete, do a quick pressure release. Carefully open the lid.
5. Divide the muffins between plates and serve warm.

Mango And Coconut Steel-cut Oats

Serves:4 | Cooking Time: 5 Minutes

Ingredients:

- 1 (13.5-ounce) can coconut milk
- 1¼ cups steel-cut oats
- Salt
- ¼ to ⅓ cup loosely packed coconut sugar or brown sugar
- 1 large mango, pitted, peeled, and diced
- ½ cup unsweetened coconut flakes, lightly toasted
- ¼ cup chopped macadamia nuts

Directions:

1. Combine the coconut milk, 1¼ cups warm water, the oats, and a generous pinch of salt in the Instant Pot. Lock on the lid, select the PRESSURE COOK function, and adjust to HIGH pressure for 13 minutes. Make sure the steam valve is in the "Sealing" position. (Or you can SLOW COOK it—see below.)
2. When the cooking time is up, let the pressure come down naturally for 15 minutes and then quick-release the remaining pressure. Stir the sugar into the oats. The oats will thicken a bit upon standing.
3. Top the oats with the mango, coconut flakes, and nuts. Serve warm.

Lemony Pancake Bites With Blueberry Syrup

Serves:4 | Cooking Time: 24 Minutes

Ingredients:

- 1 (7-ounce) packet Hungry Jack buttermilk pancake mix
- ⅔ cup whole milk
- Juice and zest of ½ medium lemon
- ⅛ teaspoon salt
- 1 cup water
- ½ cup blueberry syrup

Directions:

1. Grease a seven-hole silicone egg mold.
2. In a medium bowl, combine pancake mix, milk, lemon juice and zest, and salt. Fill egg mold with half of batter.
3. Add water to the Instant Pot and insert steam rack. Place filled egg mold on steam rack. Lock lid.
4. Press the Manual or Pressure Cook button and adjust time to 12 minutes. When timer beeps, quick-release pressure until float valve drops. Unlock lid.
5. Allow pancake bites to cool, about 3 minutes until cool enough to handle. Pop out of mold. Repeat with remaining batter.
6. Serve warm with syrup for dipping.

Strawberry Quinoa

Serves:4 | Cooking Time: 12 Mins

Ingredients:

- 2¼ cups water
- 2 tbsps. honey
- 2 cups chopped strawberries
- ¼ tsp. pumpkin pie spice
- 1 ½ cups quinoa

Directions:

1. In the Instant Pot, mix the quinoa with honey, water, spice, and strawberries. Stir to combine.
2. Lock the lid. Select the Manual mode and set the cooking time for 2 minutes at High Pressure.
3. Once cooking is complete, do a natural pressure release for 10 minutes, then release any remaining pressure. Carefully open the lid.
4. Let the quinoa rest for 10 minutes. Give a good stir and serve immediately.

Brown Rice And Chickpeas Medley

Serves:4 | Cooking Time: 25 Mins

Ingredients:

- 1½ cups brown rice
- 1 tbsp. olive oil
- 1 cup chickpeas
- 14 oz. tomatoes, chopped
- 1 red onion, chopped

Directions:

1. Set your Instant Pot to Sauté and heat the olive oil.
2. Add the onions, stir, and cook for 3 minutes until translucent.
3. Add the tomatoes, chickpeas, and rice, and stir well.
4. Lock the lid. Select the Manual mode and cook for 20 minutes at Low Pressure.
5. Once cooking is complete, do a natural pressure release for 10 minutes, then release any remaining pressure. Carefully open the lid.
6. Let the mixture cool for 5 minutes before serving.

Strawberry Jam

Serves:6 | Cooking Time: 30 Minutes

Ingredients:

- 1 lb strawberries, chopped
- 1 cup sugar
- ½ lemon, juiced and zested
- 1 tbsp mint, chopped

Directions:

1. Add the strawberries, sugar, lemon juice, and zest to the Instant Pot. Seal the lid, select manual, and cook for 2 minutes on High.
2. Release pressure naturally for 10 minutes. Open the lid and stir in chopped mint. Select Sauté and continue cooking until the jam thickens, about 10 minutes. Let to cool before serving

Espresso Oatmeal

Serves:4 | Cooking Time: 10 Mins

Ingredients:

- 1 tsp. espresso powder
- 2½ cups water
- 2 tbsps. sugar
- 1 cup milk
- 1 cup steel-cut oats

Directions:

1. Add all the ingredients to the Instant Pot and stir well.
2. Lock the lid. Select the Manual mode and cook for 6 minutes at High Pressure.
3. Once cooking is complete, do a natural pressure release for 5 minutes. Carefully open the lid.
4. Stir your oatmeal again, divide into bowls and serve warm.

Pumpkin And Apple Butter

Serves:6 | Cooking Time: 10 Mins

Ingredients:

- 30 oz. pumpkin purée
- 4 apples, cored, peeled, and cubed
- 12 oz. apple cider
- 1 cup sugar
- 1 tbsp. pumpkin pie spic

Directions:

1. In the Instant Pot, stir together the pumpkin purée with apples, apple cider, sugar, and pumpkin pie spice.
2. Lock the lid. Select the Manual mode and cook for 10 minutes at High Pressure.
3. Once cooking is complete, do a quick pressure release. Carefully open the lid.
4. Remove from the pot and serve in bowls.

Western Omelet

Serves:4 | Cooking Time: 30 Mins

Ingredients:

- ½ cup half-and-half
- 4 chopped spring onions
- 6 whisked eggs
- ¼ tsp. salt
- 8 oz. bacon, chopped
- 1½ cups water

Directions:

1. Place the steamer basket in the Instant Pot and pour in 1½ cups water.
2. In a bowl, combine the eggs with half-and-half, bacon, spring onions and salt, and whisk well. Pour the egg mixture into a soufflé dish and transfer to the steamer basket.
3. Lock the lid. Select the Steam mode and cook for 30 minutes at High Pressure.
4. Once cooking is complete, do a quick pressure release. Carefully open the lid.
5. Allow to cool for 5 minutes before serving.

Beans & Grains Recipes

Beans & Grains Recipes

Basic Tomato Rice

Serves: 4 | Cooking Time:5 Minutes

Ingredients:

- 1 tbsp. extra virgin olive oil
- 2 cups white rice, rinsed and drained
- 4½ cups water
- 1 large, ripe tomato
- Salt and pepper, to taste

Directions:

1. Add olive oil, rice, and water to Instant Pot. Gently stir.
2. Place whole tomato, bottom-side up, in the middle.
3. Lock the lid. Select the Rice mode, then set the timer for 5 minutes at Low Pressure.
4. Once the timer goes off, do a natural pressure release for 3 to 5 minutes, then release any remaining pressure. Carefully open the lid.
5. Using a rice paddle, break up tomato while fluffing up rice. Season with salt and pepper.
6. Serve immediately.

Paprika Lima Bean And Pancetta Dip

Serves:12 | Cooking Time: 30 Minutes

Ingredients:

- 20 oz frozen lima beans
- 4 pancetta slices, cooked and crumbled
- 3 tsp butter, melted
- ½ tsp paprika
- Salt and black pepper to taste

Directions:

1. Place beans in IP and cover with water. Seal the lid and cook on Manual for 25 minutes at High. Do a quick pressure release. Transfer to a food processor along with the remaining ingredients. Process until smooth.

Kidney Beans

Serves: 4 | Cooking Time: 55 Minutes

Ingredients:

- 1 cup dried white kidney beans
- 6 cups water
- ½ tsp salt

Directions:

1. Add the beans, water and salt to the Instant Pot
2. Close and secure the lid. Select the MANUAL setting and set the cooking time for 40 minutes at HIGH pressure.
3. Once timer goes off, allow to Naturally Release for 10 minutes. Release any remaining pressure manually. Open the lid.
4. Serve as side dish.

Instant Pot Buckwheat Porridge

Serves: 4 | Cooking Time: 6 Minutes

Ingredients:

- 1 cup buckwheat groats
- 3 cups milk
- 1 banana, sliced
- ¼ cup raisins
- 1 teaspoon ground cinnamon
- ½ teaspoon vanilla
- Chopped nuts for garnish

Directions:

1. Place all ingredients except the nuts in the Instant Pot.
2. Close the lid and seal off the vent.
3. Press the Manual button and adjust the cooking time to 6 minutes.
4. Do natural pressure release.
5. Sprinkle with nuts on top.

Strawberry And Rolled Oats

Serves: 2 | Cooking Time: 10 Minutes

Ingredients:

- 2 cups water
- ⅓ cup rolled oats
- 2 tbsps. frozen dried strawberries
- ⅔ cup whole milk
- Pinch of salt
- ½ tsp. white sugar

Directions:

1. Arrange the steamer rack in the Instant Pot, then pour in the water.
2. Combine the oats, strawberries, milk, and salt in a bowl. Stir to mix well.
3. Put the bowl on the steamer rack.
4. Lock the lid. Set to the Manual mode, then set the timer for 10 minutes at High Pressure.
5. Once the timer goes off, perform a natural pressure release for 5 minutes, then release any remaining pressure. Carefully open the lid.
6. Remove the bowl from the pot, then sprinkle with sugar and serve.

Garlic & Butter Beans

Serves:6 | Cooking Time: 20 Minutes

Ingredients:

- 2 tsp olive oil
- 2 cups butter beans, soaked
- 2 cloves garlic, minced
- 1 bay leaf
- Salt and black pepper to taste

Directions:

1. Put all ingredients in IP. Pour in 4 cups of water. Select Manual and cook for 15 minutes at High. Once done, do a quick pressure release. Discard bay leaf to serve.

Gouda Cheese Bean Spread

Servings: 4 | Cooking Time: 50 Minutes

Ingredients:

- ¼ cup grated Parmesan cheese + extra for topping
- 1 cup kidney beans, soaked
- 4 cups chicken broth
- ¼ cup grated mozzarella
- ¼ cup grated Gouda cheese

Directions:

1. Pour beans and broth in your Instant Pot. Seal the lid, select Pressure Cook on High, and set to 30 minutes. After, do a natural release for 10 minutes. Stir in cheeses until melted. Spoon over toasts and top with Parmesan cheese. Serve.

Perfect Quinoa

Serves: 2-4 | Cooking Time: 15 Minutes

Ingredients:

- 2 cups quinoa
- 3 cups water or vegetable broth
- Juice of 1 lemon
- ½ tsp salt
- Handful your choice of fresh herbs, minced

Directions:

1. Rinse the quinoa well.
2. Add the quinoa, broth, lemon juice, salt, and, if using, herbs into the Instant Pot.
3. Close and secure the lid. Select MANUAL and set the cooking time for 1 minute at HIGH pressure.
4. When the timer goes off, use a Natural Release for 10 minutes, then release any remaining pressure.
5. Carefully unlock the lid and fluff the cooked quinoa with a fork.
6. Serve.

Chorizo Pinto Beans

Serves: 3 | Cooking Time: 47 Minutes

Ingredients:

- ½ tablespoon cooking oil
- 2 oz. dry Spanish) chorizo½ yellow onion1 ½ garlic cloves1 cup dry pinto beans1 bay leaf½ teaspoon freshly cracked pepper1 ½ cups chicken broth1 cup 7.1 oz.) tomatoes, diced
- Boiled white rice or tortilla chips to serve

Directions:

1. Add the oil, chorizo, garlic and onion to the Instant Pot. "Sauté" for 5 minutes.
2. Stir in beans, pepper and bay leaf. Cook for 1 minute, then add the broth.
3. Cover and secure the lid. Turn its pressure release handle to the sealing position.
4. Cook on the "Manual" function with high pressure for 35 minutes.
5. After the beep, do a Natural release for 20 minutes.

6. Stir in diced tomatoes and cook for 7 minutes on the "Sauté" setting.
7. Serve hot with boiled white rice or tortilla chips.

Bresaola & Black Eyed Peas

Serves: 4 | Cooking Time: 35 Minutes

Ingredients:

- ½ lb dried black-eyed peas
- 3 ½ cups chicken stock
- 3 oz bresaola, torn into pieces
- Salt and black pepper to taste

Directions:

1. Place the black-eyed peas and chicken stock in your Instant Pot. Seal the lid, select Manual, and cook for 30 minutes on High pressure. Once ready, allow a natural release for 20 minutes and unlock the lid. Sprinkle with salt and pepper to taste. Serve topped with bresaola.

Mexican Rice

Serves: 4 | Cooking Time: 10 Minutes

Ingredients:

- 2 cups long-grain rice
- 2½ cup water
- ½ cup green salsa
- 1 cup cilantro
- 1 avocado
- Salt and pepper, to taste

Directions:

1. Add the rice and water to the Instant Pot.
2. Lock the lid. Select the Rice mode, then set the timer for 5 minutes at Low Pressure.
3. Once the timer goes off, do a natural pressure release for 3 to 5 minutes. Carefully open the lid.
4. Fluff rice and let it cool. Put the salsa, cilantro, and avocado in a blender.
5. Pulse the ingredients together until they are creamy and mix into the rice.
6. Mix everything together and season with salt and pepper.
7. Serve immediately.

Spanish Lentejas Caseras

Servings:x | Cooking Time: 50 Minutes

Ingredients:

- 3/4 cup brown jasmine rice
- 7 cups water
- 1/2 teaspoon sea salt
- 1 cup kale, torn into pieces
- 1/2 cup yellow lentils
- Salt and ground black pepper, to taste
- 1 tablespoon pepitas, toasted

Directions:

1. Place the rice, water, and salt in the inner pot.
2. Secure the lid. Choose the "Manual" mode and cook for 25 minutes at High pressure. Once cooking is complete, use a natural pressure release for 20 minutes; carefully remove the lid.
3. Add the kale, lentils, salt, and black pepper to the inner pot.
4. Secure the lid. Choose the "Manual" mode and cook for 2 minutes at High pressure. Once cooking is complete, use a quick pressure release; carefully remove the lid.
5. Serve in individual bowls garnished with toasted pepitas.

Simple Boiled Pinto Beans

Serves: 8 | Cooking Time: 45 Minutes

Ingredients:

- 1-pound dry pinto beans, rinsed
- 5 ½ cups water
- 1 2/3 tablespoons vegetable bullion

Directions:

1. Place all ingredients in the Instant Pot.
2. Close the lid and seal off the vent.
3. Press the Manual button and adjust the cooking time to 45 minutes.

Millet Pudding

Serves: 2-4 | Cooking Time: 25 Minutes

Ingredients:

- 2/3 cup millet
- 1 and 2/3 cups coconut milk
- 4 dates, pitted
- Salt to taste
- 7 oz water
- Honey for serving

Directions:

1. Add the millet, milk, dates and a pinch of salt to the Instant Pot and stir well.
2. Add the water and stir again.
3. Close and secure the lid. Select MANUAL and cook at HIGH pressure for 10 minutes.
4. Once cooking is complete, use a Natural Release for 10 minutes, then release any remaining pressure.
5. Uncover the pot and fluff the dish with a fork.
6. Top with honey in the serving bowls.

Black Beans With Chorizo

Serves: 3 | Cooking Time: 47 Minutes

Ingredients:

- ½ tablespoon cooking oil
- 2 oz. dry Spanish) chorizo½ yellow onion1 ½ garlic cloves1 cup black beans, soaked and rinsed
- 1 bay leaf½ teaspoon cracked pepper1 ½ cups sodium-reduced chicken broth1 cup 7.1 oz.) tomatoes, diced
- Boiled white rice or tortilla chips to serve

Directions:

1. Add the oil, chorizo, garlic and onion to the Instant Pot. "Sauté" for 5 minutes.
2. Stir in beans, pepper and bay leaf. Cook for 1 minute, then add the chicken broth.
3. Cover and secure the lid. Turn its pressure release handle to the sealing position.
4. Cook on the "Manual" function with high pressure for 35 minutes.
5. After the beep, do a Natural release for 15-20 minutes.
6. Stir in diced tomatoes and cook for 7 minutes on the "Sauté" setting.
7. Serve hot with boiled white rice or tortilla chips.

Basic Instant Pot Millet

Serves: 4 | Cooking Time: 9 Minutes

Ingredients:

- ½ cup millet
- 1 cup water

Directions:

1. Place all ingredients in the Instant Pot.
2. Close the lid and press the Manual button.3. Adjust the cooking time to 9 minutes.

Raisin Butter Rice

Serves: 4 | Cooking Time: 12 Minutes

Ingredients:

- 3 cups wild rice, soaked in water overnight and drained
- 3 cups water
- ½ cup raisins
- ¼ cup salted butter
- 1 tsp. salt

Directions:

1. Add all the ingredients to the Instant Pot.
2. Lock the lid. Select the Rice mode, then set the timer for 12 minutes at Low Pressure.
3. Once the timer goes off, perform a natural release for 8 to 10 minutes.
4. Carefully open the lid and use a fork to fluff the rice.
5. Serve warm.

Instant Pot Rice

Serves: 8 | Cooking Time: 25 Minutes

Ingredients:

- 3 cups rice (any type)
- 3 cups water
- A dash of salt

Directions:

1. Rinse the rice under cold running water.
2. Place the rice in the Instant Pot and pour in water.
3. Season with salt.
4. Close the lid and seal off the valve.
5. Press the Rice button and adjust the cooking time depending on the type of rice you are cooking.
6. If you are cooking for white rice, set the timer for 6 minutes and 22 minutes for brown rice.

7. Do natural pressure release.
8. Fluff the rice once cooked.

Black-eyed Peas With Ham

Serves: 4 | Cooking Time: 30 Minutes

Ingredients:

- ½ lb. dried black-eyed peas
- 3 oz. ham, diced
- 3½ cups chicken stock
- Salt and ground black pepper, to taste

Directions:

1. Place the peas, ham, and chicken stock in the Instant Pot.
2. Lock the lid. Select the Manual mode and cook for 30 minutes at High Pressure.
3. Once cooking is complete, do a natural pressure release for 20 minutes, then release any remaining pressure. Carefully open the lid.
4. Season as needed with salt and pepper, then serve.

Almond Risotto

Serves: 3 | Cooking Time: 5 Minutes

Ingredients:

- 2 cups vanilla almond milk
- ½ cup Arborio short-grain Italian) rice
- 2 tablespoons agave syrup1 teaspoon vanilla extract
- ¼ cup toasted almond flakes garnish

Directions:

1. Add all the ingredients to the Instant Pot.
2. Cover and secure the lid. Turn its pressure release handle to the sealing position.
3. Cook on the "Manual" function with high pressure for 5 minutes.
4. After the beep, do a Natural release for 20 minutes.
5. Garnish with almond flakes and serve.

Khichdi Dal

Serves: 4 | Cooking Time: 12 Minutes

Ingredients:

- 1 tbsp. butter
- 2 cups water
- ¼ tsp. salt
- 1 tsp. Balti seasoning
- 1 cup khichdi mix

Directions:

1. Set the Instant Pot to Sauté. Add the butter and heat to melt.
2. Mix in the Balti seasoning and cook for 1 minute.
3. Add the Khichdi mix, water, and salt to the pot.
4. Lock the lid. Select the Porridge mode, then set the timer for 10 minutes at High Pressure.
5. Once the timer goes off, do a natural pressure release for 3 to 5 minutes. Carefully open the lid.
6. Fluff the khichdi with a fork and serve warm.

Black Eyed Peas And Ham

Serves: 4-6 | Cooking Time: 55 Minutes

Ingredients:

- ½ lb dried black-eyed peas
- 3 ½ cups chicken stock
- 3 oz ham, diced
- Salt and ground black pepper to taste

Directions:

1. Add the peas, chicken stock and ham to the Instant Pot.
2. Close and secure the lid. Select MANUAL and cook at HIGH pressure for 30 minutes.
3. Once cooking is complete, select CANCEL and let Naturally Release for 20 minutes. Open the lid.
4. Add salt and pepper to taste if needed. Serve.

Black Olives In Tomato Rice

Serves: 4 | Cooking Time:5 Minutes

Ingredients:

- ¼ tsp. balsamic vinegar
- 4½ cups water
- ¼ cup black olives in brine rings
- 1 cup ripe tomato, deseeded and minced
- 2 cups Basmati rice, rinsed and drained
- Salt and pepper, to taste

Directions:

1. Pour all the ingredients into Instant Pot. Gently stir.
2. Lock the lid. Select the Rice mode, then set the timer for 5 minutes at Low Pressure.
3. Once the timer goes off, do a natural pressure release for 3 to 5 minutes, then release any remaining pressure. Carefully open the lid.
4. Using a rice paddle, fluff up rice.
5. Serve warm.

Brothy Beans With Cream

Serves: 4 | Cooking Time: 50 Minutes

Ingredients:

- 2 cups mixed dried heirloom beans, soaked overnight
- 2 quarts chicken stock
- 4 sprigs thyme
- Salt and pepper to taste
- ½ cup heavy cream

Directions:

1. Place all ingredients in the Instant Pot except for the cream.
2. Close the lid and press the Manual button.
3. Adjust the cooking time to 45 minutes.
4. Do quick pressure release.
5. Without the lid on, press the Sauté button and add in the heavy cream.
6. Allow to simmer for 5 minutes.

Cheesy Porridge With Kale

Servings:x | Cooking Time: 20 Minutes

Ingredients:

- 1/2 cup teff grains
- 2 cups water
- 1/2 teaspoon sea salt
- 1 tablespoon olive oil
- 1 cup kale, torn into pieces
- 1/3 cup goat cheese, crumbled
- 1 tomato, sliced

Directions:

1. Place the teff grains, water, salt, and olive oil in the inner pot of your Instant Pot.
2. Secure the lid. Choose the "Manual" mode and cook for 3 minutes at High pressure. Once cooking is complete, use a quick pressure release; carefully remove the lid.
3. Add the kale and seal the lid again; let it soak for 5 to 10 minutes. Serve garnished with goat cheese and fresh tomatoes. Bon appétit!

Peaches And Steel-cut Oats

Serves: 2 | Cooking Time: 3 Minutes

Ingredients:

- 2 peaches, diced
- 1 cup steel-cut oats
- 1 cup coconut milk
- ½ vanilla bean, scraped, seeds and pod
- 2 cups water

Directions:

1. Put all the ingredients into the Instant Pot. Stir to mix well.
2. Lock the lid. Set to the Manual mode, then set the timer for 3 minutes at High Pressure.
3. Once the timer goes off, perform a quick pressure release. Carefully open the lid.
4. Serve immediately.

Basic Instant Pot Risotto

Serves: 6 | Cooking Time:5 Minutes

Ingredients:

- 2 cups Arborio rice
- 4 cups chicken broth
- 1 onion, chopped
- 1 swig of white wine
- 1 tablespoon parmesan cheese, grated
- Salt and pepper to taste

Directions:

1. Press the Sauté button on the Instant Pot.
2. Place the rice, half of the chicken broth, onion, and wine.
3. Allow simmering for 3 minutes.4. The rice should turn from solid white to translucent.
4. Pour the rest of the chicken broth and stir in the parmesan cheese. Season with salt and pepper to taste.
5. Close the lid.
6. Press the Manual button and adjust the cooking time to 4 minutes.
7. Do natural pressure release.
8. Press the Sauté button and allow to simmer until the right thickness.

Multigrain Rice

Serves: 6 To 8 | Cooking Time: 20 Minutes

Ingredients:

- 2 tbsps. olive oil
- 3¾ cups water
- 3 cups wild brown rice
- Salt, to taste

Directions:

1. Combine the oil, water, and brown rice in the pot.
2. Season with salt.
3. Lock the lid. Select the Multigrain mode, then set the timer for 20 minutes on Low Pressure.
4. Once the timer goes off, do a natural pressure release for 5 minutes. Carefully open the lid.
5. Fluff the rice with a fork.
6. Serve immediately.

Lentil Chili

Serves: 6-8 | Cooking Time: 40 Minutes

Ingredients:

- 1 tbsp olive oil
- 1 onion, diced
- 28 oz canned diced tomatoes, undrained
- 2 cups lentils
- 6 cups vegetable broth

Directions:

1. Select the SAUTÉ setting on the Instant Pot and heat the oil.
2. Add the onion and sauté for about 5 minutes, until softened.
3. Add the tomatoes and sauté for 1 minute more.
4. Add the lentils and broth and stir.
5. Close and lock the lid. Select MANUAL and cook at HIGH pressure for 18 minutes.
6. Once cooking is complete, let the pressure Release Naturally for 15 minutes. Release any remaining steam manually.
7. Open the lid and gently stir. Serve.

Instant Pot Coconut Oatmeal

Serves: 2 | Cooking Time: 3 Minutes

Ingredients:

- 1 cup steel-cut oats
- 2 cups water
- 1 cup coconut milk
- ½ cup coconut sugar
- 1 apple, cored and sliced

Directions:

1. Place all ingredients in the Instant Pot.
2. Stir to combine.
3. Close the lid and press the Manual button.4. Adjust the cooking time to 3 minutes.
4. Do natural pressure release.

Pakistani Jeera Rice

Servings:x | Cooking Time: 30 Minutes

Ingredients:

- 3/4 cup rice basmati rice, rinsed
- 1/2 cup water
- 1 cup cream of celery soup
- 1/2 green chili deveined and chopped
- Sea salt and ground black pepper, to taste
- 1 bay leaf
- 1/2 teaspoon Jeera (cumin seeds)
- 1 tablespoon sesame oil

Directions:

1. Place all ingredients in the inner pot. Stir until everything is well combined.
2. Secure the lid. Choose the "Rice" mode and cook for 10 minutes at Low pressure. Once cooking is complete, use a natural pressure release for 15 minutes; carefully remove the lid.
3. Serve with Indian main dishes of choice. Enjoy!

Pinto Bean & Beet Hummus

Servings: 4 | Cooking Time: 20 Minutes

Ingredients:

- ¼ cup olive oil
- 2 large beets, peeled, chopped
- 2 cups canned pinto beans
- 2 cups vegetable stock
- 1 tsp garlic powder
- ½ lemon, juiced

Directions:

1. Combine beets, drained pinto beans, vegetable stock, and garlic powder into your Instant Pot. Seal the lid, select Pressure Cook on High, and set the time to 13 minutes.

2. After cooking, do a quick release and unlock the lid. Transfer mixture to a blender and process until smooth. Add lemon juice and olive oil and blend again to combine. Pour mixture into bowls and serve.

Brothy Heirloom Beans With Cream

Serves: 4 | Cooking Time: 45 Minutes

Ingredients:

- 2 cups mixed dried heirloom beans, soaked overnight
- 8 cups chicken stock
- 4 sprigs thyme
- Salt, to taste
- ½ cup heavy cream

Directions:

1. Add the beans, chicken stock, thyme, and salt to the Instant Pot. Stir well.

2. Lock the lid. Select the Manual mode and set the cooking time for 45 minutes at High Pressure.

3. Once cooking is complete, do a quick pressure release. Carefully open the lid.

4. Set your Instant Pot to Sauté and stir in the heavy cream.

5. Allow to simmer for 5 minutes, then transfer to four bowls. Serve warm.

Bulgur Pilau With Shallots

Servings:x | Cooking Time: 25 Minutes

Ingredients:

- 1 tablespoon butter
- 2 shallots, chopped
- 1 teaspoon fresh garlic, minced
- 1/2 cup bulgur wheat
- 1 cup vegetable broth
- 1/4 teaspoon ground black pepper
- 1/4 teaspoon fine sea salt

Directions:

1. Press the "Sauté" button and melt the butter. Now, cook the shallots until just tender and fragrant.

2. Then, stir in the garlic and continue to sauté an additional minute or so. Add the remaining ingredients to the inner pot.

3. Secure the lid. Choose the "Manual" mode and cook for 10 minutes at High pressure. Once cooking is complete, use a natural pressure release for 10 minutes; carefully remove the lid.

4. Fluff the bulgur wheat with a fork and serve immediately. Bon appétit!

Cinnamon Almond Oatmeal

Servings:4 | Cooking Time: 15 Minutes

Ingredients:

- 1 ½ cups regular oats
- 2 cups water
- 2 cups almond milk
- 1 teaspoon cinnamon, ground
- 2 tablespoons almond butter
- 1/2 cup chocolate chips

Directions:

1. Simply throw the oats, water, milk, and cinnamon into the Instant Pot.

2. Secure the lid. Choose the "Manual" mode and High pressure; cook for 10 minutes. Once cooking is complete, use a quick pressure release; carefully remove the lid.

3. Divide the oatmeal between serving bowls; top with almond butter and chocolate chips. Enjoy!

Stewed Tomatoes And Green Beans

Serves: 4-6 | Cooking Time: 15 Minutes

Ingredients:

- 1 tsp olive oil
- 1 clove garlic, crushed
- 2 cups fresh, chopped tomatoes
- ½ cup water
- 1 lb trimmed green beans
- Salt to taste

Directions:

1. Select the SAUTÉ setting on the Instant Pot and heat the oil.

2. Add the garlic and sauté until fragrant and golden. Add tomatoes and stir. If the tomatoes are dry, add ½ cup water.

3. Put the green beans in the Instant Pot and sprinkle with salt.
4. Close and secure the lid. Select MANUAL and cook at HIGH pressure for 5 minutes.
5. Once pressure cooking is complete, use a Quick Release.
6. If the beans aren't quite tender enough, sauté in sauce for a few minutes. Serve.

Ham And Peas

Serves: 8-10 | Cooking Time: 50 Minutes

Ingredients:

• 2 cups dried peas, use black-eyed (rinse, but do not pre-soak)
• 3 oz ham, diced
• 3½ cups stock (vegetable, chicken or 3¼ cups water mixed with 2 tbsp chicken bouillon)
• Salt and ground black pepper to taste

Directions:

1. Add the peas, ham and stock to the Instant Pot and stir.
2. Close and lock the lid. Select the MANUAL setting and set the cooking time for 30 minutes at HIGH pressure.
3. When the timer goes off, let the pressure Release Naturally for 10 minutes, then release any remaining steam manually. Carefully unlock the lid.
4. Add salt and pepper to taste if needed. Serve

Easy Cheesy Polenta

Servings:4 | Cooking Time: 15 Minutes

Ingredients:

• 6 cups roasted vegetable broth
• 1/2 stick butter, softened
• 1 ½ cups cornmeal
• Sea salt and ground black pepper, to taste
• 1 cup Cheddar cheese, shredded
• 1/2 cup Ricotta cheese, at room temperature

Directions:

1. Press the "Sauté" button to preheat the Instant Pot. Then, add the broth and butter; bring to a boil. Slowly and gradually, whisk in the cornmeal. Season with the salt and pepper.
2. Secure the lid. Choose the "Manual" mode and High pressure; cook for 8 minutes. Once cooking is complete, use a natural pressure release; carefully re-move the lid.
3. Divide between individual bowls; serve topped with cheese. Bon appétit!

Fig Millet

Serves: 4-6 | Cooking Time: 25 Minutes

Ingredients:

• 1¾ cups millet
• 1 cup almond milk
• 2 cups water
• 1/3 cup chopped dried figs
• 2 tbsp coconut oil

Directions:

1. Add the millet, milk, water, figs and coconut oil to the Instant Pot and stir.
2. Close and secure the lid. Select the SOUP setting and set the cooking time for 10 minutes.
3. When the timer goes off, let the pressure Release Naturally for 10 minutes, then release any remaining steam.
4. Fluff the dish with a fork. Serve.

Basic Instant Pot Quinoa

Serves: 6 | Cooking Time: 12 Minutes

Ingredients:

• 1 cup quinoa, rinsed
• 2 cups water

Directions:

1. Place all ingredients in the Instant Pot.
2. Close the lid and seal off the vent.
3. Press the Manual button and adjust the cooking time to 12 minutes.
4. Do natural pressure release.

Breakfast Millet Porridge With Nuts

Servings:x | Cooking Time: 25 Minutes

Ingredients:

• 3/4 cup millet
• 2 cups water
• 1/4 cup golden raisins
• 1/4 cup almonds, roughly chopped
• 1 tablespoon orange juice
• A pinch of sea salt

Directions:

1. Place all ingredients in the inner pot of your Instant Pot and close the lid.
2. Secure the lid. Choose the "Manual" mode and cook for 12 minutes at High pressure. Once cooking is complete, use a natural pressure release for 10 minutes; carefully remove the lid.
3. Taste and adjust the seasonings. Bon appétit!

Creamy Polenta

Serves: 2 | Cooking Time: 8 Minutes

Ingredients:

- 2⅓ cups milk, divided
- ½ tsp. salt
- ½ cup polenta
- 3 tbsps. butter

Directions:

1. Set the pot to Sauté and add 2 cups of milk and bring it to a boil.
2. Add the salt and polenta into the milk.
3. Lock the lid. Select the Porridge mode, then set the timer for 8 minutes at High Pressure.
4. Once the timer goes off, do a natural pressure release for 5 minutes. Carefully open the lid.
5. Stir in the remaining milk and butter, then serve.

Classic Navy Beans

Servings:6 | Cooking Time: 35 Minutes

Ingredients:

- 1 ¼ pounds dry navy beans
- 6 cups water
- 2 tablespoons bouillon granules
- 2 bay leaves
- 1 teaspoon black peppercorns, to taste

Directions:

1. Rinse off and drain navy beans. Place navy beans, water, bouillon granules, bay leaves, and black peppercorns in your Instant Pot.
2. Secure the lid. Choose the "Manual" mode and cook at High pressure for 20 minutes.
3. Once cooking is complete, use a natural release; remove the lid carefully. Bon appétit!

Quinoa And Blueberry

Serves: 2-4 | Cooking Time: 15 Minutes

Ingredients:

- 1½ cups quinoa
- 1½ cups water
- 1 tbsp honey
- 1 cup apple juice
- 3 tbsp blueberries

Directions:

1. Rinse the quinoa well.
2. In the instant pot, add quinoa and water, stir until well combined.
3. Close and secure the lid. Select MANUAL and cook at HIGH pressure for 1 minute.
4. Once cooking is complete, use a Natural Release for 10 minutes, then release any remaining pressure.
5. Open the pot. Add honey, apple juice and blueberries, stir well. Serve

Authentic Sushi Rice

Servings:x | Cooking Time: 30 Minutes

Ingredients:

- 1 cup sushi rice, rinsed
- 1 cup water
- 2 tablespoons rice vinegar
- 1/2 tablespoon brown sugar
- 1/2 teaspoon salt
- 1 tablespoon soy sauce

Directions:

1. Place the sushi rice and water in the inner pot of your Instant Pot.
2. Secure the lid. Choose the "Rice" mode and cook for 10 minutes at Low pressure. Once cooking is complete, use a natural pressure release for 15 minutes; carefully remove the lid.
3. Meanwhile, whisk the rice vinegar, sugar, salt and soy sauce in a mixing dish; microwave the sauce for 1 minute.
4. Pour the sauce over the sushi rice; stir to combine. Assemble your sushi rolls and enjoy!

Coconut Risotto

Serves: 3 | Cooking Time: 5 Minutes

Ingredients:

- 2 cups coconut milk
- ½ cup Arborio short-grain Italian) rice
- 2 tablespoons coconut sugar1 teaspoon vanilla extract
- ¼ cup toasted coconut flakes garnish

Directions:

1. Add all the ingredients to the Instant Pot.
2. Cover and secure the lid. Turn its pressure release handle to the sealing position.
3. Cook on the "Manual" function with high pressure for 5 minutes.
4. After the beep, do a Natural release for 20 minutes.
5. Garnish with coconut flakes and serve.

Black Currant-coconut Rye Porridge

Servings: 2 | Cooking Time: 20 Minutes

Ingredients:

- 1 cup rye flakes
- A pinch of salt
- 1 ¼ cups coconut milk
- 1 tsp vanilla extract
- 2 tbsp maple syrup
- ¾ cup frozen black currants

Directions:

1. In your Instant Pot, combine rye flakes, salt, coconut milk, water, vanilla, and maple syrup. Seal the lid, select Pressure Cook on High, and set the time to 5 minutes. After cooking, perform a natural pressure release for 10 minutes. Stir and spoon porridge into serving bowls. Top with black currants and serve warm.

Truffle And Parmesan Popcorn

Servings:x | Cooking Time: 15 Minutes

Ingredients:

- 1/2 stick butter
- 1/2 cup popcorn kernels
- 1 tablespoon truffle oil
- 1/4 cup parmesan cheese, grated
- Sea salt, to taste

Directions:

1. Press the "Sauté" button and melt the butter. Stir until it begins to simmer.
2. Stir in the popcorn kernels and cover. When the popping slows down, press the "Cancel" button.
3. Now, add the truffle oil, parmesan, and sea salt. Toss to combine and serve immediately.

Amaranth Pilaf With Eggs And Cheese

Servings:x | Cooking Time: 15 Minutes

Ingredients:

- 3/4 cup amaranth
- 2 cups water
- 1/2 cup milk
- Sea salt and freshly cracked black pepper, to taste
- 1 tablespoon olive oil
- 2 eggs
- 1/2 cup cheddar cheese, shredded
- 2 tablespoons fresh chives, roughly chopped

Directions:

1. Place the amaranth, water, and milk in the inner pot of your Instant Pot.
2. Secure the lid. Choose the "Manual" mode and cook for 4 minutes at High pressure. Once cooking is complete, use a quick pressure release; carefully remove the lid. Season with salt and black pepper.
3. Meanwhile, heat the oil in a skillet over medium-high heat. Then, fry the egg until crispy on the edges.
4. Divide the cooked amaranth between serving bowls; top with the fried eggs and cheese. Garnish with fresh chives. Bon appétit!

Poultry Recipes

Poultry Recipes

Lemon Garlic Chicken

Serves: 6 | Cooking Time: 12 Minutes

Ingredients:

- 3 tbsps. olive oil, divided
- 2 tsps. dried parsley
- 6 chicken breasts
- 3 minced garlic cloves
- 1 tbsp. lemon juice
- Salt and pepper, to taste

Directions:

1. Mix together 2 tablespoons olive oil, chicken breasts, parsley, garlic cloves, and lemon juice in a large bowl. Place in the refrigerator to marinate for 1 hour.
2. Press the Sauté button on the Instant Pot and heat the remaining olive oil.
3. Cook the chicken breasts for 5 to 6 minutes per side until cooked through.
4. Allow to cool for 5 minutes before serving.

Chicken Nachos

Serves: 6 | Cooking Time: 45 Minutes

Ingredients:

- 2 lbs chicken thighs, boneless, skinless
- 1 tbsp olive oil
- 1 package (1 oz) taco seasoning mix
- 2/3 cup mild red salsa
- 1/3 cup mild Herdez salsa verde

Directions:

1. Select the SAUTÉ setting on the Instant Pot and heat the oil.
2. Add the chicken thighs and brown the meat nicely for a few minutes on each side.
3. In a medium bowl, combine the taco seasoning and salsa.
4. Pour the mixture in the pot and stir well. Close and lock the lid.
5. Press the CANCEL button to reset the cooking program, then select the MANUAL setting and set the cooking time for 15 minutes at HIGH pressure.
6. Once cooking is complete, use a Natural Release for 10 minutes, then release any remaining pressure

manually. Uncover the pot.
7. Shred the meat. Serve with tortilla chips.

Cajun Chicken With Snow Beans

Serves:4 | Cooking Time: 35 Minutes

Ingredients:

- 4 chicken breasts
- 2 cups snow beans, frozen
- 14 oz cornbread stuffing
- 1 tsp cajun seasoning
- 1 cup chicken broth
- Salt and black pepper to taste

Directions:

1. Add chicken and broth to your IP, seal the lid and cook on Poultry for 20 minutes at High. Do a quick pressure release. Add the snow beans, seal the lid again, and cook for 2 more minutes on Manual at High. Do a quick release, stir in the cornbread stuffing, and Cajun seasoning and cook for another 5 minutes on Sauté, lid off. Serve hot.

Simple Sage Whole Chicken

Serves:4 | Cooking Time: 35 Minutes

Ingredients:

- 1 (3-lb) whole chicken
- 2 tbsp olive oil
- Salt and black pepper to taste
- 2 fresh sage, chopped

Directions:

1. Season chicken all over with salt and pepper. Heat the oil on Sauté and cook the chicken until browned on all sides. Set aside and wipe clean the cooker. Insert a rack in your pressure cooker and pour in 1 cup of water. Lower the chicken onto the rack. Seal the lid, press Poultry and cook for 25 minutes at High. Once ready, do a quick pressure release. Let cool for a few minutes, slice, and sprinkle with sage to serve.

Orange & Red Pepper Infused Chicken

Serves:4 | Cooking Time: 35 Minutes

Ingredients:

- 2 tsp red pepper flakes
- 1 cup orange-tangerine juice
- 4 chicken breasts, halved
- 1/3 cup honey
- Salt and black pepper to taste
- Chopped cilantro for garnish

Directions:

1. Coat your IP with cooking spray and add in the chicken breasts. In a bowl, mix together the remaining ingredients until well combined. Pour the mixture over the chicken breasts along with a cup of water. Seal the lid, select Manual at High, and cook for 20 minutes. When ready, release the pressure naturally for 5 minutes. Serve hot, sprinkled with flesh cilantro.

Rosemary Whole Chicken With Asparagus Sauce

Serves: 4 | Cooking Time: 40 Minutes

Ingredients:

- 1 (3 ½ lb) young whole chicken
- 4 garlic cloves, minced
- 1 tsp olive oil
- 4 fresh thyme, minced
- 3 fresh rosemary, minced
- 2 lemons, zested and quartered
- Salt and black pepper to taste
- 2 tbsp olive oil
- 8 oz asparagus, trimmed and chopped
- 1 onion, chopped
- 1 cup chicken stock
- 1 tbsp soy sauce
- 1 fresh thyme sprig
- 1 tbsp flour
- Chopped parsley to garnish

Directions:

1. Rub all sides of the chicken with garlic, rosemary, black pepper, lemon zest, thyme, and salt. Into the chicken cavity, insert lemon wedges. Warm oil on Sauté. Add in onion and asparagus, and Sauté for 5 minutes until softened. Mix chicken stock, 1 thyme sprig, black pepper, soy sauce, and salt.

2. Into the inner pot, set trivet over asparagus mixture. On top of the trivet, place the chicken with breast-side up. Seal the lid, select Poultry and cook for 20 minutes on High Pressure. Do a quick release. Remove the chicken to a serving platter.

3. In the inner pot, sprinkle flour over asparagus mixture and blend the sauce with an immersion blender until desired consistency. Top the chicken with asparagus sauce and garnish with parsley.

Onion Chicken With Salsa Verde

Serves: 2-4 | Cooking Time: 35 Minutes

Ingredients:

- 1 large yellow onion, chopped
- 1 cup salsa verde
- ½ cup chicken broth
- Salt and black pepper to taste
- 4 chicken breasts, cut into 1-inch cubes

Directions:

1. In inner pot, combine onion, salsa verde, chicken broth, salt, black pepper, and chicken. Seal the lid, select Manual on High, and set cooking time to 12 minutes.

2. After cooking, perform a natural pressure release for 10 minutes. Unlock the lid and remove chicken onto a plate and serve warm over salad.

Party Bbq Chicken

Serves: 2-4 | Cooking Time:40 Minutes

Ingredients:

- 1 ½ cups chopped sweet pineapple
- ¼ cup chicken broth
- ¼ tsp salt
- ¾ cup BBQ sauce
- 4 chicken breasts, cut into 1-inch cubes

Directions:

1. In inner pot, combine pineapples, chicken broth, salt, BBQ sauce, and chicken. Seal the lid, select Manual on High, and set cooking time to 12 minutes. After cooking, perform a natural pressure release for 10 minutes, then a quick pressure release to let out remaining steam, and unlock the lid. Remove chicken onto a plate and select Sauté. Cook sauce until boiled down by half, 4 minutes, and stir in chicken. Serve.

Garlicky Greek Chicken

Serves:6 | Cooking Time: 12 Mins

Ingredients:

- 1 tsp. dried oregano
- 1 sliced lemon
- 3 tbsps. extra-virgin olive oil
- 1 lb. chicken thighs
- 3 minced garlic cloves
- ½ cup of water
- Salt and pepper, to taste

Directions:

1. Put all the ingredients in the Instant Pot and stir well.
2. Lock the lid. Select the Poultry mode and cook for 12 minutes at High Pressure.
3. Once cooking is complete, do a natural pressure release for 6 minutes, then release any remaining pressure. Carefully open the lid.
4. Let the chicken thighs cool for 5 minutes, then serve.

Shredded Chicken Breast

Serves: 4 | Cooking Time: 30 Minutes

Ingredients:

- 1.5-2 lbs boneless chicken breasts
- ½ tsp ground black pepper
- ½ tsp garlic salt
- ½ cup chicken broth

Directions:

1. Season all sides of the chicken with the black pepper and salt.
2. Add the chicken breasts to the Instant Pot and pour the chicken broth.
3. Close and lock the lid. Select MANUAL and cook at HIGH pressure for 8 minutes.
4. Once cooking is complete, use a Natural Release for 10 minutes, then release any remaining pressure manually.
5. Remove the chicken from the pot and shred it with 2 forks. Serve.

Greek-style Cheesy Chicken

Serves: 2 | Cooking Time: 30 Minutes

Ingredients:

- ½ lb boneless skinless chicken drumsticks
- ½ cup hot tomato salsa
- ½ onion, chopped
- ⅓ cup feta cheese, crumbled

Directions:

1. Sprinkle salt over the chicken; and set in the instant pot. Stir in salsa to coat the chicken. Seal the lid and cook for 15 minutes on High Pressure. Do a quick Pressure release. Press Sauté and cook for 5 minutes as you stir until excess liquid has evaporated. Top with feta cheese and serve.

Chinese Steamed Chicken

Serves:6 | Cooking Time: 10 Mins

Ingredients:

- 1 tsp. grated ginger
- 1½ lbs. chicken thighs
- 1 tbsp. five-spice powder
- ¼ cup soy sauce
- 3 tbsps. sesame oil
- 1 cup water
- Salt and pepper, to taste

Directions:

1. In the Instant Pot, stir in all the ingredients.
2. Lock the lid. Select the Poultry mode and set the cooking time for 10 minutes at High Pressure.
3. Once cooking is complete, do a natural pressure release for 7 minutes, then release any remaining pressure. Carefully open the lid.
4. Serve the chicken thighs while warm.

Chicken Peas Rice

Serves:4 | Cooking Time: 15 Mins

Ingredients:
- 1 chopped small onion
- 4 oz. chicken breasts
- 2 cups white rice
- 1 tsp. olive oil
- ½ cup green peas
- 2 cups water

Directions:

1. Press the Sauté button on the Instant Pot and heat the oil.
2. Add the chicken breasts and sauté for 6 to 7 minutes until lightly browned. Set aside on a plate.
3. Add the onions and cook 3 to 4 minutes until translucent.
4. Add the rice, 2 cups water, and green peas, and mix well.
5. Lock the lid. Select the Manual mode and cook for 4 minutes at Low Pressure.
6. Once cooking is complete, do a natural pressure release for 5 minutes, then release any remaining pressure. Carefully open the lid.
7. Serve the rice with the chicken breasts.

Sticky Sesame Chicken Wings

Servings: 4 | Cooking Time: 25 Minutes

Ingredients:
- 2 tbsp sesame oil
- 2 lb chicken wings
- 2 tbsp hot garlic sauce
- 2 tbsp honey
- 2 garlic cloves, minced
- 1 tbsp toasted sesame seeds

Directions:

1. Pour 1 cup of water into the inner pot and insert a trivet. Place the chicken wings on the trivet. Seal the lid, select Pressure Cook on High, and set the time to 10 minutes. After cooking, do a quick pressure release. Remove the trivet and discard the water. In a large bowl, whisk the sesame oil, hot garlic sauce, honey, and garlic. Toss the wings in the sauce and put them in the pot. Press Sauté and cook for 5 minutes. Sprinkle with the sesame seeds to serve.

Smoky Paprika Chicken

Serves: 6 | Cooking Time: 15 Minutes

Ingredients:
- 2 tbsps. smoked paprika
- 2 lbs. chicken breasts
- Salt and pepper, to taste
- 1 tbsp. olive oil
- ½ cup water

Directions:

1. Press the Sauté button on the Instant Pot and heat the olive oil.
2. Stir in the chicken breasts and smoked paprika and cook for 3 minutes until lightly golden.
3. Season with salt and pepper and add ½ cup water.
4. Lock the lid. Select the Manual mode and cook for 12 minutes at High Pressure.
5. Once cooking is complete, do a natural pressure release for 8 minutes, then release any remaining pressure. Carefully open the lid.
6. Garnish with cilantro or scallions, if desired.

Classic Lemon Chicken

Serves:4 | Cooking Time: 10 Mins

Ingredients:
- 4 chicken thighs
- 2 tbsps. fresh lemon juice
- 1 medium red onion, sliced
- 2 tsps. olive oil
- 1 garlic clove, crushed
- 1 cup water

Directions:

1. Line a baking pan with parchment paper and set aside.
2. In a mixing bowl, thoroughly mix olive oil and lemon juice. Add the chicken thighs and toss to coat. Transfer to the baking pan and top with the garlic and onion slices.
3. Pour 1 cup water into the Instant Pot. Arrange a steamer basket inside it and place the baking pan on the basket.
4. Lock the lid. Select the Manual mode and cook for 6 minutes at High Pressure.
5. Once cooking is complete, do a quick pressure release. Carefully open the lid.
6. Allow to cool for 5 minutes before serving.

Spiced Chicken Drumsticks

Serves: 10 To 12 | Cooking Time: 15 Minutes

Ingredients:

- ¼ tsp. dried thyme
- 1½ tbsps. paprika
- Salt and pepper, to taste
- ½ tsp. onion powder
- 12 chicken drumsticks
- 2 cups water

Directions:

1. On a clean work surface, rub the chicken drumsticks generously with the spices. Season with salt and pepper.
2. Transfer the chicken to the Instant Pot and add the water.
3. Lock the lid. Select the Poultry mode and cook for 15 minutes at High Pressure.
4. Once cooking is complete, do a natural pressure release for 8 minutes, then release any remaining pressure. Carefully open the lid.
5. Remove from the pot to a plate and serve.

Broccoli & Turkey Barley With Gouda

Servings: 4 | Cooking Time: 25 Minutes

Ingredients:

- 1 cup pearl barley
- 2 cups chicken broth
- Salt and black pepper to taste
- 1 lb turkey breasts, cubed
- 1 broccoli head, cut into florets
- 1 ½ cups shredded gouda

Directions:

1. Place the broth, pearl barley, salt, pepper, and turkey in your Instant Pot. Seal the lid, select Manual/Pressure Cook on High, and set the time to 10 minutes. When done, perform a quick pressure release and unlock the lid. Press Sauté and add the broccoli; cook for 4 minutes. Scatter shredded gouda cheese over the top and serve.

Cajun Chicken With Zucchini

Serves: 6 | Cooking Time: 10 To 15 Minutes

Ingredients:

- 1 lb. skinless chicken drumsticks
- ½ tsp. Cajun seasoning
- 1 small red bell pepper, sliced
- 1½ tsps. olive oil, divided
- 1 small zucchini, sliced

Directions:

1. Select the Sauté mode and heat 1 teaspoon olive oil.
2. Add the chicken drumsticks and bell pepper and cook for 4 to 5 minutes per side until evenly browned. Transfer to a plate and set aside.
3. Heat the remaining olive oil in the Instant Pot.
4. Add the zucchini slices and Cajun and sauté for 2 to 3 minutes until crisp.
5. Remove from the pot and serve the chicken with zucchini on a plate.

Garlicky Chicken

Serves: 4 | Cooking Time: 15 Minutes

Ingredients:

- 5 garlic cloves, minced
- 4 chicken breasts, halved
- 3 tbsps. coconut oil
- Salt and pepper, to taste
- 1 cup water

Directions:

1. Press the Sauté button on the Instant Pot and heat the coconut oil. Sauté the garlic for 3 minutes until fragrant, then stir in the chicken breasts. Sprinkle pepper and salt for seasoning. Pour in the water.
2. Lock the lid. Select the Manual mode and cook for 6 minutes at High Pressure.
3. Once cooking is complete, do a natural pressure release for 5 minutes, then release any remaining pressure. Carefully open the lid.
4. Serve the chicken while warm.

Garlic Chicken

Serves: 4 | Cooking Time: 25 Minutes

Ingredients:

- 1 lb chicken breasts
- Salt and black pepper to taste
- 2 tbsp butter
- 1 cup chicken broth
- 2 garlic cloves, minced
- 2 tbsp tarragon, chopped

Directions:

1. Place chicken breasts in your Instant Pot. Sprinkle with garlic, salt, and pepper. Pour in the chicken broth and butter. Seal the lid, select Manual, and cook for 15 minutes on High pressure. When over, allow a natural release for 10 minutes and unlock the lid. Remove the chicken and shred it. Top with tarragon and serve.

Salsa Verde Chicken

Serves: 6 | Cooking Time: 25 Minutes

Ingredients:

- 2½ lbs boneless chicken breasts
- 1 tsp smoked paprika
- 1 tsp cumin
- 1 tsp salt
- 2 cup (16 oz) salsa verde

Directions:

1. Add the chicken breasts, paprika, cumin, and salt to the Instant Pot.
2. Pour the salsa verde on top.
3. Close and lock the lid. Select the MANUAL setting and set the cooking time for 20 minutes at HIGH pressure.
4. Once pressure cooking is complete, use a Quick Release. Unlock and carefully open the lid.
5. Shred the meat. Serve.

Egg Muffins

Serves: 2 | Cooking Time: 15 Minutes

Ingredients:

- 4 beaten eggs
- 4 bacon slices, cooked and crumbled
- 4 tbsp cheddar cheese, shredded
- 1 green onion, chopped
- A pinch of salt
- 1½ cups water

Directions:

1. In a medium bowl, whisk together eggs, bacon, cheese, onion and salt until combined.
2. Divide the mixture into muffin cups.
3. Pour the water into the Instant Pot and insert a steamer basket.
4. Place the muffin cups in the basket.
5. Close and lock the lid. Select MANUAL and cook at HIGH pressure for 8 minutes.
6. When the timer goes off, allow a 2 minutes rest time and then do a Quick Release.
7. Carefully unlock the lid. Remove the steamer basket with muffins from the pot. Serve.

Chili Lime Chicken

Serves:5 | Cooking Time: 12 Mins

Ingredients:

- 6 garlic cloves, minced
- 1 tbsp. chili powder
- 1 tsp. cumin
- 1 lb. skinless and boneless chicken breasts
- 1 ½ limes, juiced
- 1 cup wate

Directions:

1. In the Instant Pot, add the chicken breasts, garlic, chili powder, cumin, lime juice, salt, pepper, and water.
2. Lock the lid. Select the Manual mode and cook for 6 minutes at High Pressure.
3. Once cooking is complete, do a natural pressure release for 5 minutes, then release any remaining pressure. Carefully open the lid.
4. Cool for 5 minutes and serve warm.

Cashew Chicken With Sautéed Vegetables

Serves: 6 | Cooking Time: 20 Minutes

Ingredients:

- 2 lbs. chicken breasts, thinly sliced
- Salt and pepper, to taste
- 1 head broccoli florets
- 1 cup cubed red bell pepper
- 1 cup cashew nuts, toasted
- ½ cup water

Directions:

1. Press the Sauté button on the Instant Pot. Stir in the chicken breasts and cook for 5 minutes. Sprinkle pepper and salt for seasoning. Pour in ½ cup water for additional moisture.

2. Press the Poultry button and set the cooking time for 10 minutes at High Pressure.

3. Once cooking is complete, do a quick pressure release. Carefully open the lid. Transfer the chicken breast to a large plate.

4. Press the Sauté button and stir in the broccoli and red bell pepper. Allow to simmer for 5 minutes. Scatter the toasted cashew nuts over the vegetables.

5. Serve the chicken breasts with sautéed vegetables on the side.

Fabulous Orange Chicken Stew

Serves: 4 | Cooking Time: 50 Minutes

Ingredients:

- 2 lb chicken breast, boneless and skinless
- 1 cup fire-roasted tomatoes, diced
- 1 tbsp chili powder
- Salt and white pepper to taste
- 1 cup orange juice
- 2 cups chicken broth

Directions:

1. Season the chicken with salt and pepper, and place in your instant pot. Add the remaining ingredients, except for the orange juice and chicken broth, and cook on Sauté mode for 10 minutes, stirring occasionally.

2. Press Cancel, pour in the broth and orange juice. Seal the lid and cook on Poultry for 25 minutes on High. Release the pressure naturally, for 10 minutes. Serve immediately.

Saucy Orange Chicken

Serves: 4 | Cooking Time: 30 Minutes

Ingredients:

- 4 chicken breasts
- ¼ cup ketchup
- ¾ cup orange marmalade
- ½ cup soy sauce
- 2 tbsp green onions, chopped

Directions:

1. Place chicken breasts, 1 cup of water, ketchup, orange marmalade, and soy sauce in your Instant Pot and stir. Seal the lid and cook for 15 minutes on Poultry. When ready, perform a quick pressure release and unlock the lid. Simmer for 5 minutes on Sauté until the sauce thickens. Top with green onions and serve.

Broccoli Chicken With Parmesan

Serves: 2 To 3 | Cooking Time: 5 Minutes

Ingredients:

- ⅓ cup grated Parmesan cheese
- 1 cup chicken broth
- 2 cups broccoli florets
- ½ cup heavy cream
- 3 cups cooked and shredded chicken
- Salt and pepper, to taste

Directions:

1. In the Instant pot, add the broth, broccoli, chicken, salt, and pepper. Using a spatula, stir the ingredients.

2. Lock the lid. Select the Steam mode and cook for 3 minutes at High Pressure.

3. Once cooking is complete, do a quick pressure release. Carefully open the lid.

4. Set your Instant Pot to Sauté and stir in the cream.

5. Cook for 2 minutes. Transfer to a large plate and serve.

Hot Chicken Wings With Sage

Serves:16 | Cooking Time: 30 Minutes

Ingredients:

- 16 chicken wings
- 1 cup hot sauce
- ½ cup chicken broth
- 2 tbsp butter
- 1 tbsp sage
- Salt and black pepper to taste

Directions:

1. Add all ingredients with 1 cup of water in your IP, and seal the lid. Cook on Manual for 15 minutes at High. When ready, press Cancel and release pressure naturally for 10 minutes. Serve hot.

Chicken Yogurt Salsa

Serves: 4 | Cooking Time: 15 Minutes

Ingredients:

- 1 medium jar salsa
- ½ cup water
- 1 cup plain Greek yogurt
- 4 chicken breasts

Directions:

1. Add all the ingredients to the Instant Pot. Using a spatula, gently stir to combine well.
2. Lock the lid. Select the Poultry mode and set the cooking time for 15 minutes at High Pressure.
3. Once cooking is complete, do a natural pressure release for 8 minutes, then release any remaining pressure. Carefully open the lid.
4. Transfer the cooked mixture to a salad bowl and serve warm.

Chicken Breasts With Caraway Seeds

Serves:4 | Cooking Time: 35 Minutes

Ingredients:

- 2 lb chicken breasts
- 1 cup celery, chopped
- 1 tbsp caraway seeds
- 1 carrot, chopped
- 2 ¼ cups vegetable stock
- Salt and black pepper to taste

Directions:

1. Chop the chicken into small pieces and place in your IP. Add the remaining ingredients and stir well to combine. Seal the lid and cook on Manual for 15 minutes at High. When ready, release pressure naturally for 10 minutes. Season with salt and pepper and serve.

Saucy Enchilada Chicken

Servings: 4 | Cooking Time: 20 Minutes

Ingredients:

- 1 cup chicken broth
- 4 chicken breasts, cubed
- 1 ½ tsp dried oregano
- 1 ½ tsp cumin powder
- 1 ½ cups red enchilada sauce

Directions:

1. In your Instant Pot, combine broth, chicken, oregano, cumin, and enchilada sauce. Seal the lid, select Pressure Cook on High, and set the cooking time to 10 minutes. After cooking, perform a natural pressure release for 5 minutes, then a quick pressure release to let out the remaining steam. Unlock the lid, stir, and serve the chicken with sauce.

Instant Pot Emergency Broccoli Chicken

Serves: 4 | Cooking Time: 10 Minutes

Ingredients:

- ¼ cup soy sauce
- 1 head broccoli florets
- 1 tbsp. coconut oil
- 1½ lbs. chicken breasts, sliced
- 3 minced garlic cloves

Directions:

1. Press the Sauté button on the Instant Pot and heat the oil. Sauté the garlic until fragrant, about 2 minutes.
2. Stir in the chicken breasts, broccoli florets, and soy sauce.
3. Lock the lid. Select the Manual mode and cook for 8 minutes at High Pressure.
4. Once cooking is complete, do a natural pressure release for 5 minutes, then release any remaining pressure. Carefully open the lid.
5. Serve the chicken with broccoli florets on a plate.

Simple Omelet Cups

Serves: 2 | Cooking Time 25 Minutes

Ingredients:

- ½ tsp olive oil
- 3 eggs, beaten
- 1 cup water
- Salt and freshly ground black pepper to taste
- 1 onion, chopped
- 1 jalapeño pepper, chopped

Directions:

1. Prepare two ramekins by adding a drop of olive oil in each and rubbing the bottom and sides.
2. In a medium bowl, whisk together the eggs, water, salt and black pepper until combined.
3. Add the onion and jalapeño, stir.
4. Transfer egg mixture to the ramekins.
5. Prepare the Instant Pot by adding the water to the pot and placing the steam rack in it.
6. Place the ramekins on the steam rack and secure the lid.
7. Close and lock the lid. Select MANUAL and cook at HIGH pressure for 5 minutes.
8. When the timer goes off, use a Quick Release. Carefully unlock the lid.
9. Serve hot.

Bell Pepper Egg Cups

Serves: 4 | Cooking Time: 20 Minutes

Ingredients:

- 4 bell peppers
- 4 eggs
- Salt and ground black pepper to taste
- 2/3 cup water
- 2 tbsp mozzarella cheese, grated freshly
- Chopped fresh herbs

Directions:

1. Cut the bell peppers ends to form about 1½-inch high cup. Remove the seeds.
2. Crack 1 egg into each pepper. Season with salt and black pepper. Cover each bell pepper with a piece of foil.
3. Pour the water into the Instant Pot and insert a steamer basket.
4. Place the bell peppers in the basket.
5. Close and lock the lid. Select MANUAL and cook at HIGH pressure for 4 minutes.

6. When the timer goes off, use a Quick Release. Carefully unlock the lid.
7. Transfer the bell pepper cups onto serving plates.
8. Sprinkle with mozzarella cheese and chopped fresh herbs of your choice. Serve.

Root Beer Chicken Wings

Serves: 8 | Cooking Time: 15 Minutes

Ingredients:

- 2 pounds chicken wings
- 2 cans of root beer
- ¼ cup sugar
- ¼ cup soy sauce

Directions:

1. Place all ingredients in the Instant Pot.
2. Give a good stir.
3. Close the lid and press the Poultry button. 4. Adjust the cooking time to 10 minutes.
4. Do quick pressure release.

Chimichurri Chicken

Serves: 6 | Cooking Time: 25 Minutes

Ingredients:

- 2 lb chicken breasts
- 1 cup chicken broth
- 1 tsp smoked paprika
- 1 tsp cumin
- Salt and black pepper to taste
- 2 cups chimichurri salsa

Directions:

1. Sprinkle chicken breasts with paprika, cumin, salt, and pepper. Place the chicken broth with chicken breasts in your Instant Pot. Seal the lid, select Manual, and cook for 15 minutes on High pressure. Once done, perform a quick pressure release and unlock the lid. Cut the chicken into slices and top with chimichurri sauce. Serve immediately.

Quinoa Pilaf With Chicken

Serves: 4 | Cooking Time: 40 Minutes

Ingredients:

- 1 lb chicken breasts, boneless, skinless
- 1 cup quinoa
- 2 cups chicken broth
- Salt and black pepper to taste
- Greek yogurt for topping

Directions:

1. Add chicken and broth to the pot and seal the lid. Cook on Poultry for 15 minutes on High. Do a quick release and remove the chicken. Add quinoa and seal the lid. Cook on Rice mode for 8 minutes on High.

2. Meanwhile, cut the chicken meat into bite-sized pieces and place in a large bowl. To the cooker, do a quick release. Stir in chicken, to warm, season with salt, black pepper and, top with greek yogurt.

Garlic Chicken With Lemongrass

Serves: 2-4 | Cooking Time: 40 Minutes

Ingredients:

- 2 lemongrass stalks, chopped
- 2 garlic cloves, minced
- Salt and black pepper to taste
- 1 cup chicken broth
- 4 chicken breasts
- 1 lemon, juiced

Directions:

1. In inner pot, combine lemongrass, garlic, salt, pepper, chicken broth, and chicken. Seal the lid, select Manual on High, and set cooking time to 12 minutes.

2. After cooking, perform a natural pressure release for 10 minutes, then a quick pressure release to let out remaining steam, and unlock the lid. Select Sauté and remove chicken onto a plate. Take out lemongrass and discard. Shred chicken into strands and return to sauce. Stir in lemon juice and cook further for 5 minutes. Serve warm.

Instant Pot Pesto Chicken

Serves: 4 | Cooking Time: 10 Minutes

Ingredients:

- 4 chicken breasts
- ¼ cup extra virgin olive oil
- Salt and pepper, to taste
- 2 cups basil leaves
- 5 sun-dried tomatoes
- 1 cup water, if needed

Directions:

1. Put the basil leaves, olive oil, and tomatoes in the food processor until smooth. Season with salt and people to taste. Add a cup of water if needed.

2. Place the chicken in the Instant Pot. Pour the sauce over the chicken.

3. Lock the lid. Select the Manual mode and cook for 8 minutes at High Pressure.

4. Once cooking is complete, do a natural pressure release for 6 minutes, then release any remaining pressure. Carefully open the lid.

5. Transfer to a large plate and serve warm.

Fish & Seafood Recipes

Fish & Seafood Recipes

Red Curry Halibut

Serves: 4 | Cooking Time: 10 Minutes

Ingredients:

- 2 tbsps. chopped cilantro
- 4 skinless halibut fillets
- 3 green curry leaves
- 1 cup chopped tomatoes
- 1 tbsp. freshly squeezed lime juice
- Salt and pepper, to taste

Directions:

1. Place all ingredients in the Instant Pot. Give a good stir to combine the ingredients.
2. Lock the lid. Select the Manual mode and cook for 10 minutes at Low Pressure.
3. Do a quick pressure release.

Tasty Crab Legs

Serves: 4-6 | Cooking Time: 10 Minutes

Ingredients:

- 4 lbs king crab legs, broken in half
- 1 cup water
- ¼ cup butter
- 3 lemon wedges

Directions:

1. Pour the water into the Instant Pot and insert a steamer basket.
2. Place the crab legs on the rack.
3. Close and lock the lid. Select MANUAL and cook at HIGH pressure for 3 minutes.
4. When the timer goes off, use a Quick Release. Carefully open the lid.
5. Transfer the legs to a serving bowl; add melted butter and lemon wedges. Serve.

Mussels With White Wine

Serves: 4 | Cooking Time: 15 Minutes

Ingredients:

- 3 lbs mussels, cleaned and debearded
- 6 tbsp butter
- 4 shallots, chopped
- 1 cup white wine
- 1½ cups chicken stock

Directions:

1. Add the butter to the Instant Pot and select SAUTÉ.
2. Once the butter has melted, add the shallots and sauté for 2 minutes.
3. Pour in the wine, stir and cook for another 1 minute.
4. Add the stock and mussels, stir well. Close and lock the lid.
5. Press the CANCEL button to stop the SAUTE function, then select the MANUAL setting and set the cooking time for 3 minutes at HIGH pressure.
6. Once pressure cooking is complete, use a Quick Release. Unlock and carefully open the lid.
7. Remove unopened mussels and serve.

Savory Crab Legs

Serves:4 | Cooking Time: 12 Minutes

Ingredients:

- 2 lb king crab legs
- 2 tbsp parsley, chopped
- 2 tbsp butter, melted
- 2 garlic cloves, minced
- 4 lemon wedges

Directions:

1. Pour 1 cup of water into the IP and insert a trivet. Break the crab legs in half and place on the trivet. Seal the lid, select Manual at High, and cook for 4 minutes. When done, release the pressure naturally for 5 minutes. In a bowl, combine butter, parsley, and garlic and pour the mixture over crab legs. Serve with lemon wedges.

Mediterranean Tuna Steaks

Serves: 2 | Cooking Time: 10 Minutes

Ingredients:

- 4 tbsp olive oil
- 2 tuna steaks
- Salt and black pepper to taste
- 1 lemon, zested and lemon juice
- 2 tbsp chopped thyme + extra for garnishing
- 3 tbsp drained capers

Directions:

1. Pour 1 cup of water in inner pot and fit in trivet. Season tuna with 1 tbsp of olive oil, salt, black pepper, and arrange on trivet. Seal the lid, select Manual/Pressure Cook mode on High, and set cooking time to 6 minutes.
2. After cooking, do a quick pressure release. Remove fish to a serving platter. Empty and clean inner pot. Set the pot to Sauté and heat remaining olive oil. Sauté lemon zest, lemon juice, thyme, capers, and 2 tbsp of water. Cook for 3 minutes. Pour sauce over tuna and garnish with thyme.

Effortless Seafood Jambalaya

Servings: 4 | Cooking Time: 25 Minutes

Ingredients:

- 2 tbsp olive oil
- 1 onion, chopped
- 2 cups chicken broth
- 1 cup white rice, long-grain
- ½ lb shrimp, deveined
- 2 andouille sausages, sliced

Directions:

1. Heat the olive oil in the Instant Pot on Sauté. Cook sausage and onion for 5 minutes. Pour in broth and rice and stir.
2. Seal the lid, select Pressure Cook, and set the time to 8 minutes. Once cooking is complete, perform a quick release. Press Sauté and stir in the shrimp. Cook for 3 minutes. Serve and enjoy!

Simple Curried Shrimps

Serves: 4 | Cooking Time: 4 Minutes

Ingredients:

- 1 tbsp. extra virgin olive oil
- 1½ lb. raw shrimp, peeled and deveined
- 2 oranges, peeled and separated
- 1 tbsp. curry powder
- Salt and pepper, to taste

Directions:

1. Press the Sauté button on the Instant Pot and heat the olive oil.
2. Toast the curry powder for a minute until fragrant. Add the shrimps and oranges. Sprinkle salt and pepper for seasoning.
3. Lock the lid. Select the Manual mode and cook for 4 minutes at Low Pressure.
4. Once cooking is complete, do a quick pressure release. Carefully open the lid.
5. Serve warm.

Mussels With Butter-scallion Sauce

Servings:x | Cooking Time: 10 Minutes

Ingredients:

- 1/2 cup water
- 1/2 cup cooking wine
- 1 garlic clove, sliced
- 1 pound frozen mussels, cleaned and debearded
- 1 tablespoon butter
- 2 tablespoons fresh scallion, chopped

Directions:

1. Add the water, wine, and garlic to the inner pot. Add a metal rack to the inner pot.
2. Put the mussels into the steamer basket; lower the steamer basket onto the rack.
3. Secure the lid. Choose the "Steam" mode and cook for 3 minutes at Low pressure. Once cooking is complete, use a quick pressure release; carefully remove the lid.
4. Press the "Sauté" button and add butter and scallions; let it cook until the sauce is thoroughly heated and slightly thickened. Press the "Cancel" button and add the mussels. Serve warm. Bon appétit!

Fast Shrimp Scampi

Serves: 4 | Cooking Time: 4 Minutes

Ingredients:

- 1 cup chicken stock
- 2 tbsps. butter
- Juice of 1 lemon
- 1 lb. shrimp, peeled and deveined
- 2 shallots, chopped

Directions:

1. Set the Instant Pot on Sauté mode, add butter, heat it up.
2. Add shallots and sauté for 1 to 2 minutes.
3. Add shrimp, lemon juice and stock, stir.
4. Lock the lid. Select the Manual mode and cook for 2 minutes at Low Pressure.
5. Once cooking is complete, do a quick pressure release. Carefully open the lid.
6. Divide into bowls and serve.

Mussels With Lemon & White Wine

Serves: 5 | Cooking Time: 15 Minutes

Ingredients:

- 1 cup white wine
- ½ cup water
- 1 tsp garlic powder
- 2 pounds mussels, cleaned and debearded
- Juice from 1 lemon

Directions:

1. In the pot, mix garlic powder, water and wine. Put the mussels into the steamer basket, rounded-side should be placed facing upwards to fit as many as possible.
2. Insert rack into the cooker and lower steamer basket onto the rack. Seal the lid and cook on Low Pressure for 1 minute. Release the pressure quickly. Remove unopened mussels. Coat the mussels with the wine mixture and lemon juice to serve.

Buttery Steamed Lobster Tails

Serves: 6 | Cooking Time: 3 Minutes

Ingredients:

- 1 cup water
- ¾ lb. lobster tails, halved
- ½ tsp. red pepper flakes
- Sea salt and freshly ground black pepper, to taste
- ¼ stick butter, at room temperature

Directions:

1. Add the water and steamer basket to your Instant Pot. Arrange the lobster tails (shell-side down) in the steamer basket.
2. Lock the lid. Select the Steam mode and set the cooking time for 3 minutes at Low Pressure.
3. Once cooking is complete, do a quick pressure release. Carefully open the lid.
4. Remove the lobster tails from the pot to a large plate.
5. Sprinkle with the red pepper flakes, salt, and black pepper. Spread the butter over the lobster tails and serve.

Dijon Salmon

Serves: 2 | Cooking Time: 15 Minutes

Ingredients:

- 2 fish fillets or steaks, such as salmon, cod, or halibut (1-inch thick)
- 1 cup water
- Salt and ground black pepper to taste
- 2 tsp Dijon mustard

Directions:

1. Pour the water into the Instant Pot and insert a steam rack.
2. Sprinkle the fish with salt and pepper.
3. Place the fillets on the rack skin-side down and spread the Dijon mustard on top of each fillets or steaks.
4. Close and lock the lid. Select MANUAL and cook at HIGH pressure for 5 minutes.
5. When the timer goes off, use a Quick Release. Carefully open the lid.

Cheddar Creamy Haddock

Serves: 3 | Cooking Time: 10 Minutes

Ingredients:
- 12 oz. haddock fillets
- 3 tbsps. diced onions
- 1 tbsp. butter
- Salt and pepper, to taste
- ½ cup heavy cream
- 5 oz. grated Cheddar cheese

Directions:
1. Heat the Instant Pot on Sauté mode.
2. Add the butter and onions to the Instant Pot. Sauté until onions become translucent and softened, 3 minutes.
3. Season the fish with salt and pepper. Add the fish in the pot and cook for 2 minutes per side.
4. Add the cream and the cheese.
5. Lock the lid. Select the Manual mode and cook for 5 minutes at Low Pressure.
6. Once cooking is complete, do a quick pressure release. Carefully open the lid.
7. Serve immediately.

Cod With Orange Sauce

Serves: 4 | Cooking Time: 7 Minutes

Ingredients:
- 1 cup white wine
- 1 small ginger piece, grated
- 4 spring onions, finely chopped
- Juice of 1 orange
- 4 boneless cod fillets

Directions:
1. In the Instant Pot, combine the wine with ginger, spring onions and orange juice, stir, add steamer basket, add cod fillets inside.
2. Lock the lid. Select the Manual mode, then set the timer for 7 minutes at Low Pressure.
3. Once the timer goes off, do a quick pressure release. Carefully open the lid.
4. Divide fish on plates, drizzle orange juice all over and serve.

Boiled Garlic Clams

Serves: 4 | Cooking Time: 6 Minutes

Ingredients:
- 1 cup water
- ½ cup freshly chopped parsley
- 2 tbsps. olive oil
- 6 garlic cloves
- 50 scrubbed small clams
- Salt and pepper, to taste

Directions:
1. Press the Sauté button on the Instant Pot and heat the olive oil. Sauté the garlic until fragrant and slightly browned.
2. Add the clams, water, and parsley. Sprinkle salt and pepper for seasoning.
3. Lock the lid. Select the Manual mode and cook for 6 minutes at Low Pressure.
4. Once cooking is complete, do a quick pressure release. Carefully open the lid.
5. Serve warm.

Salmon With Basil Pesto

Serves: 6 | Cooking Time: 6 Minutes

Ingredients:
- 3 garlic cloves, minced
- 1½ lbs. salmon fillets
- 2 cups basil leaves
- 2 tbsps. freshly squeezed lemon juice
- ½ cup olive oil
- Salt and pepper, to taste

Directions:
1. Make the pesto sauce: Put the basil leaves, olive oil, lemon juice, and garlic in a food processor, and pulse until smooth.
2. Season with salt and pepper.
3. Place the salmon fillets in the Instant Pot and add the pesto sauce.
4. Lock the lid. Select the Manual mode and set the cooking time for 6 minutes at Low Pressure.
5. Once cooking is complete, do a quick pressure release. Carefully open the lid.
6. Divide the salmon among six plates and serve.

Dilled Salmon Fillets

Serves: 4 | Cooking Time: 25 Minutes

Ingredients:

- 4 salmon fillets
- 1 cup lemon juice
- 2 tbsp butter, softened
- 2 tbsp dill
- Salt and black pepper to taste

Directions:

1. Sprinkle the fillets with salt and pepper. Insert the steamer tray and place the salmon on top. Pour in the lemon juice and 2 cups of water. Seal the lid.
2. Cook on Steam mode for 5 minutes on High. When done, release the Pressure naturally, for 10 minutes. Set aside the salmon and discard the liquid.
3. Wipe the pot clean and press Sauté. Add butter and briefly brown the fillets on both sides – for 3-4 minutes. Sprinkle with dill, to serve.

Simple Instant Pot Salmon

Serves: 2 | Cooking Time: 10 Minutes

Ingredients:

- 2 salmon fillets
- Salt and pepper

Directions:

1. Place a trivet or steamer basket in the Instant Pot.
2. Pour a cup of water.
3. Season the salmon fillets with salt and pepper to taste.
4. Place on the steamer salmon fillets.
5. Close the lid and press the Steam button.
6. Adjust the cooking time to 10 minutes.
7. Do natural pressure release.

Spicy Sockeye Salmon

Serves: 4 | Cooking Time: 15 Minutes

Ingredients:

- 4 wild sockeye salmon fillets
- 2 tbsp assorted chili pepper seasoning
- Salt and ground black pepper to taste
- ¼ cup lemon juice
- 1 cup water

Directions:

1. Season the salmon fillets with chili pepper, salt,

pepper, and lemon juice.
2. Pour the water into the Instant Pot and insert a steamer basket.
3. Place the fillets in the basket.
4. Close and lock the lid. Select MANUAL and cook at HIGH pressure for 5 minutes.
5. When the timer goes off, use a quick release. Carefully open the lid.
6. Serve.

Steamed Pollock

Serves:4 | Cooking Time: 24 Minutes

Ingredients:

- 4 Alaskan pollock fillets
- 1 tsp sea salt
- 1 lemon, sliced
- 2 tbsp parsley, chopped

Directions:

1. Add 1 cup of water to the IP and insert a trivet. Place the pollock on the trivet. Seal the lid, select Manual at High, and cook for 6 minutes. When done, release the pressure naturally for 5 minutes. Serve topped with parsley, sea salt and lemon slices.

Easy White Wine Mussels

Serves: 2-4 | Cooking Time: 15 Minutes

Ingredients:

- 1 cup white wine
- ½ cup water
- 1 tsp garlic powder
- 2 pounds mussels, cleaned and debearded
- Juice from 1 lemon

Directions:

1. In the pot, mix garlic powder, water and wine.
2. Put the mussels into the steamer basket, rounded-side should be placed facing upwards to fit as many as possible.
3. Insert rack into the cooker and lower steamer basket onto the rack. Seal the lid and cook on Low Pressure for 1 minute. Release the pressure quickly.
4. Remove unopened mussels. Coat the mussels with the wine mixture. Serve with a side of French fries or slices of toasted bread.

Cod And Orange Sauce

Serves: 4 | Cooking Time: 15 Minutes

Ingredients:

- 4 cod fillets, boneless
- A small ginger piece, grated
- 1 cup white wine
- Juice from 1 orange
- Salt and ground black pepper to taste.
- 4 spring onions, chopped

Directions:

1. Add the ginger, wine, and orange juice to the Instant Pot, mix well,
2. Place a steamer basket on top.
3. Place the cod fillets in the basket. Season with salt and pepper.
4. Close and lock the lid. Select MANUAL and cook at HIGH pressure for 7 minutes.
5. When the timer goes off, use a Quick Release. Carefully open the lid.
6. Serve the fish with sauce and sprinkle with green onions.

Tuna Fillets With Eschalots

Servings:4 | Cooking Time: 10 Minutes

Ingredients:

- 2 lemons, 1 whole and 1 freshly squeezed
- 1 pound tuna fillets
- Sea salt and ground black pepper, to taste
- 1 tablespoon dried parsley flakes
- 2 tablespoons butter, melted
- 2 eschalots, thinly sliced

Directions:

1. Place 1 cup of water and lemon juice in the Instant Pot. Add a steamer basket too.
2. Place the tuna fillets in the steamer basket. Sprinkle the salt, pepper, and parsley over the fish; drizzle with butter and top with thinly sliced eschalots.
3. Secure the lid. Choose the "Steam" mode and Low pressure; cook for 3 minutes. Once cooking is complete, use a quick pressure release; carefully remove the lid.
4. Serve immediately with lemon. Bon appétit!

Steamed Herbed Red Snapper

Serves: 4 | Cooking Time: 12 Minutes

Ingredients:

- 1 cup water
- 4 red snapper fillets
- 1½ tsps. chopped fresh herbs
- ¼ tsp. paprika
- 3 tbsps. freshly squeezed lemon juice
- Salt and pepper, to taste

Directions:

1. Set a trivet in the Instant Pot and pour the water into the pot.
2. Mix all ingredients in a heat-proof dish that will fit in the Instant Pot. Combine to coat the fish with all ingredients.
3. Place the heat-proof dish on the trivet.
4. Lock the lid. Select the Manual mode and cook for 12 minutes at Low Pressure.
5. Once cooking is complete, do a quick pressure release. Carefully open the lid.
6. Serve warm.

Nut Crusted Tilapia

Serves:4 | Cooking Time: 15 Minutes

Ingredients:

- 4 tilapia fillets
- ⅔ cup cashews, crushed
- 2 tbsp Dijon mustard
- 1 tsp olive oil
- Black pepper to taste
- 1 tbsp dill

Directions:

1. Pour 1 cup of water in the pressure cooker and place in a trivet. Mix olive oil, black pepper, dill and mustard in a small bowl. Brush the fish fillets with the mustard mixture on all sides. Coat the fish in cashews. Arrange the fish fillets on top of the trivet. Seal lid, select Manual for 10 minutes at High. When done, do a quick pressure release.

Smoked Codfish With Scallions

Serves: 3 | Cooking Time: 10 Minutes

Ingredients:

- 1 lemon, sliced
- 1/2 cup water
- 3 fillets smoked codfish
- 3 teaspoons butter
- 3 tablespoons scallions, chopped
- Sea salt and ground black pepper, to taste

Directions:

1. Place the lemon and water in the bottom of the Instant Pot. Place the steamer rack on top.
2. Place the cod fish fillets on the steamer rack. Add the butter, scallions, salt, and black pepper.
3. Secure the lid. Choose the "Steam" mode and cook for 3 minutes at Low pressure. Once cooking is complete, use a quick pressure release; carefully remove the lid.
4. Serve warm and enjoy!

Mahi-mahi With Tomatoes

Serves: 3 | Cooking Time: 14 Minutes

Ingredients:

- 3 4 oz.) mahi-mahi fillets1 ½ tablespoons butter
- ½ yellow onion, sliced
- ½ teaspoon dried oregano
- 1 tablespoon fresh lemon juice
- Salt and freshly ground black pepper, to taste
- 1 14 oz.) can sugar-free diced tomatoes

Directions:

1. Add the butter to the Instant Pot. Select the "Sauté" function on it.
2. Add all the ingredient to the pot except the fillets. Cook them for 10 minutes.
3. Press the "Cancel" key, then add the mahi-mahi fillets to the sauce.
4. Cover the fillets with sauce by using a spoon.
5. Secure the lid and set the "Manual" function at high pressure for 4 minutes.
6. After the beep, do a Quick release then remove the lid.
7. Serve the fillets with their sauce, poured on top.

Wild Alaskan Cod With Cherry Tomatoes

Serves: 4 | Cooking Time: 8 Minutes

Ingredients:

- 1 large wild Alaskan Cod fillet
- 1 cup chopped cherry tomatoes
- Salt and pepper, to taste
- 2 tbsps. butter

Directions:

1. Except for the butter, add all the ingredients to the Instant Pot.
2. Lock the lid. Select the Manual mode and set the cooking time for 8 minutes at Low Pressure.
3. Once cooking is complete, do a quick pressure release. Carefully open the lid.
4. Stir in the butter and serve warm.

Clams And Corn

Serves: 6 | Cooking Time: 10 Minutes

Ingredients:

- 1-pound clams, scrubbed
- 2 corns on the cob, halved
- ½ cup dry white wine
- 4 cloves of garlic, minced
- 1 cup water

Directions:

1. Place all ingredients in the Instant Pot.
2. Close the lid and press the Manual button.
3. Adjust the cooking time to 10 minutes.
4. Do natural pressure release.

Instant Pot Salmon Fillet

Serves: 2 | Cooking Time: 10 Minutes

Ingredients:

- 2 salmon fillets, skin on
- 2 teaspoon chipotles paste
- A handful of asparagus spears, trimmed
- 1 lemon, sliced

Directions:

1. Place a trivet or steamer basket in the Instant Pot.
2. Pour a cup of water.
3. Season the salmon fillets with chipotle paste.4. Place on the steamer the asparagus and place the salmon fillets on top.

4. Arrange the lemon slices.
5. Close the lid and press the Steam button.
6. Adjust the cooking time to 10 minutes.
7. Do natural pressure release.

Blue Crab With Lemon And Herbs

Servings:x | Cooking Time: 15 Minutes

Ingredients:

- 1 pound frozen blue crab
- 1/2 cup water
- 1/3 cup dry white wine
- Sea salt and ground black pepper, to taste
- 1 sprig rosemary
- 1 sprig thyme
- 1/2 lemon, cut into wedges

Directions:

1. Add the frozen crab legs, water, wine, salt, black pepper, rosemary, and thyme to the inner pot.
2. Secure the lid. Choose the "Manual" mode and cook for 3 minutes at High pressure. Once cooking is complete, use a quick pressure release; carefully remove the lid.
3. Serve warm, garnished with fresh lemon wedges. Bon appétit!

Easy Mahi Mahi With Enchilada Sauce

Serves: 2 | Cooking Time: 8 Minutes

Ingredients:

- 2 fresh Mahi Mahi fillets
- ¼ cup commercial enchilada sauce
- Salt and pepper, to taste
- 2 tbsps. butter

Directions:

1. Add all the ingredients, except for the butter, to the Instant Pot.
2. Lock the lid. Select the Manual mode and cook for 8 minutes at Low Pressure.
3. Once cooking is complete, do a quick pressure release. Carefully open the lid.
4. Stir in the butter and serve on plates.

Delicious And Simple Octopus

Serves: 4 | Cooking Time: 15 Minutes

Ingredients:

- ¼ tsp. sweet paprika
- 2 lbs. octopus, rinsed
- Salt and black pepper, to taste
- ¼ tsp. chili powder

Directions:

1. Season octopus with salt and pepper, add to the Instant Pot.
2. Add enough water to cover, then add chili powder and paprika, stir a bit.
3. Lock the lid. Select the Manual mode and cook for 15 minutes at Low Pressure.
4. Once cooking is complete, do a quick pressure release. Carefully open the lid.
5. Cut the octopus and serve.

Spicy Lemon Halibut

Serves: 4 | Cooking Time: 8 Minutes

Ingredients:

- 4 halibut fillets
- 2 lemons, sliced
- 2 tablespoon chili pepper flakes
- Salt and pepper

Directions:

1. Place a trivet or steamer basket in the Instant Pot.
2. Pour a cup of water.
3. Season the halibut fillets with chili pepper flakes, salt, and pepper.
4. Place on the trivet and arrange slices of lemons.
5. Close the lid and press the Manual button.
6. Adjust the cooking time to 8 minutes.
7. Do natural pressure release.

Cod Meal

Serves: 2 | Cooking Time: 5 Minutes

Ingredients:

- 1 cup water
- 2 tbsps. ghee
- 1 fresh large fillet cod
- Salt and pepper, to taste

Directions:

1. Cut fillet into 3 pieces. Coat with the ghee and season with salt and pepper.
2. Pour the water into the pot and place steamer basket/trivet inside.
3. Arrange the fish pieces over the basket/trivet.
4. Lock the lid. Select the Manual mode and cook for 5 minutes at Low Pressure.
5. Once cooking is complete, do a quick pressure release. Carefully open the lid.
6. Serve warm.

Old Bay Crab

Serves: 5 | Cooking Time:15 Minutes

Ingredients:

- 1 teaspoon Old Bay seasoning
- 1 ½ pounds crabs
- 2 cloves garlic, minced
- 1 lemon, sliced
- 1 stick butter

Directions:

1. Place 1 cup water and a metal trivet in the bottom of your Instant Pot.
2. Lower the crabs onto the trivet.
3. Secure the lid. Choose the "Steam" mode and cook for 3 minutes at Low pressure. Once cooking is complete, use a quick pressure release; carefully remove the lid. Reserve.
4. Press the "Sauté" button and melt butter. Once hot, sauté the garlic and Old Bay seasoning for 2 to 3 minutes or until fragrant and thoroughly heated.
5. Add the cooked crabs and gently stir to combine. Serve with lemon slices. Bon appétit!

Chili Steamed Salmon

Serves: 2 | Cooking Time: 30 Minutes

Ingredients:

- 2 salmon fillets
- 1 red chilli, chopped
- 1 tsp sesame oil
- Salt and black pepper to taste

Directions:

1. Pour 1 cup of water in your Instant Pot and fit in a trivet. Sprinkle salmon with salt and pepper and place it on the trivet. Seal the lid and cook for 6 minutes on Steam. Once ready, allow a natural release for 10 minutes and unlock the lid. Drizzle with sesame oil and top with red chili. Serve with lemon wedges.

Lemon And Dill Fish Packets

Serves: 2 | Cooking Time: 15 Minutes

Ingredients:

- 2 tilapia fillets
- Salt and pepper
- 2 sprigs fresh dill
- 4 slices of lemon
- 2 tablespoons butter

Directions:

1. Lay a large parchment paper on a surface.
2. Place the fillet in the middle of the parchment paper.3. Season with salt and pepper. Add fresh dill and lemon slices on top.
3. Place the butter.
4. Place a trivet or a steamer basket in the Instant Pot.
5. Close the lid and press the Steam button.
6. Adjust the cooking time to 15 minutes.
7. Do quick pressure release.

Steamed Chili-rubbed Tilapia

Serves: 4 | Cooking Time: 10 Minutes

Ingredients:

- 1 cup water
- ½ tsp. garlic powder
- 1 lb. skinless tilapia fillet
- 2 tbsps. extra virgin olive oil
- Salt and pepper, to taste
- 2 tbsps. chili powder

Directions:

1. Set a trivet in the Instant Pot and pour the water into the pot.
2. Season the tilapia fillets with salt, pepper, chili powder, and garlic powder. Drizzle with olive oil on top.
3. Place in the steamer basket.
4. Lock the lid. Select the Steam mode and cook for 10 minutes at Low Pressure.
5. Once cooking is complete, do a quick pressure release. Carefully open the lid.
6. Serve warm.

Salmon With Orange Zest

Serves: 2 | Cooking Time: 17 Minutes

Ingredients:

- 2 salmon fillets
- 1 cup orange juice, freshly squeezed
- 2 tbsp cornstarch
- Salt and black pepper to taste
- ½ tsp garlic, minced
- ½ tsp orange zest, freshly grated

Directions:

1. Add all ingredients and seal the lid. Cook on High pressure for 10 minutes. Do a quick pressure release.

Basil Salmon With Artichokes & Potatoes

Serves: 4 | Cooking Time: 30 Minutes

Ingredients:

- 4 salmon fillets
- 1 lb new potatoes
- 1 cup artichoke hearts, halved
- 2 tbsp butter
- Salt and black pepper to taste
- 2 tbsp basil, chopped

Directions:

1. Season the potatoes with salt and pepper. Pour 1 cup of water in your Instant Pot and fit in a trivet. Place the potatoes on the trivet and seal the lid. Select Manual and cook for 2 minutes on High pressure. Once over, perform a quick pressure release and unlock the lid. Sprinkle the salmon and artichokes with salt and pepper.
2. Put them on the trivet with the potatoes, sprinkle with basil, and seal the lid. Select Manual and cook for another 5 minutes on High pressure. Once done, allow

a natural release for 10 minutes and unlock the lid. Remove potatoes to a bowl and stir in butter until well coated. Serve the salmon with artichokes and potatoes.

Halibut And Broccoli Casserole

Serves: 6 | Cooking Time: 6 Minutes

Ingredients:

- 1 tbsp. Dijon mustard
- 1¼ cup full-fat coconut cream
- 2 tbsps. olive oil
- 1½ lbs. halibut fillets, sliced
- 1 cup broccoli florets
- Salt and pepper, to taste

Directions:

1. In the Instant Pot, add all the ingredients. Give a good stir.
2. Lock the lid. Select the Manual mode and set the cooking time for 8 minutes at Low Pressure.
3. Once cooking is complete, do a quick pressure release. Carefully open the lid.
4. Let the fish and broccoli cool for 5 minutes before serving.

Butter-dipped Lobsters

Serves: 4 | Cooking Time: 03 Minutes

Ingredients:

- 1 cup water.
- 4 lbs. lobster tails, cut in half
- 4 tablespoons unsalted butter, melted
- Salt and black pepper to taste

Directions:

1. Pour 1 cup of water into the insert of Instant pot and place trivet inside it.
2. Place all the lobster tails over the trivet with their shell side down.
3. Cover the lid and lock it. Select the "Manual" function at low pressure for 3 minutes.
4. After the beep, press cancel and do a Quick release.
5. Remove the lid and trivet from the pot.
6. Transfer the lobster to a serving plate.
7. Pour the melted butter over lobster tails to add more flavor.
8. Sprinkle some salt and pepper on top, then serve.

Old Bay Fish Tacos

Serves: 4 | Cooking Time: 8 Minutes

Ingredients:

- 2 large cod fillets
- 1 tablespoon old bay seasoning
- 1/2 cup quesadilla cheese

Directions:

1. Place a trivet or a steamer basket in the Instant Pot. Pour a cup of water.
2. Season the cod fillets with old bay seasoning.
3. Place on top of the steamer rack.
4. Close the lid and press the Steam button.
5. Adjust the cooking time to 10 minutes.
6. Do quick pressure release.
7. Serve with quesadilla cheese on top.

Sole Fillets With Pickle Mayo

Servings:4 | Cooking Time: 10 Minutes

Ingredients:

- 1 ½ pounds sole fillets
- Sea salt and ground black pepper, to taste
- 1 teaspoon paprika
- 1/2 cup mayonnaise
- 1 tablespoon pickle juice
- 2 cloves garlic, smashed

Directions:

1. Sprinkle the fillets with salt, black pepper, and paprika.
2. Add 1 ½ cups of water and a steamer basket to the Instant Pot. Place the fish in the steamer basket.
3. Secure the lid and choose "Manual" setting. Cook for 3 minutes at Low pressure. Once cooking is complete, use a quick release; carefully remove the lid.
4. Then, make the sauce by mixing the mayonnaise with pickle juice and garlic. Serve the fish fillets with the well-chilled sauce on the side. Bon appétit!

Tilapia With Basil Pesto & Rice

Serves: 2 | Cooking Time: 20 Minutes

Ingredients:

- 2 tilapia fillets
- 2 tbsp basil pesto
- ½ cup basmati rice
- Salt and black pepper to taste

Directions:

1. Place the rice and 1 cup of water in your Instant Pot andseason with salt and pepper; fit in a trivet. Place tilapia fillets in the middle of a parchment paper sheet. Top each fillet with pesto and roll all the edges to form a packet. Place it on the trivet and seal the lid.
2. Select Manual and cook for 6 minutes on Low pressure. Once ready, perform a quick pressure release and unlock the lid. Fluff the rice with a fork and transfer to a plate. Top with tilapia and serve.

Steamed Fish Patra Ni Maachi

Serves: 4 | Cooking Time: 10 Minutes

Ingredients:

- 1-pound tilapia fillets
- ½ cup green commercial chutney

Directions:

1. Place a trivet or a steamer basket in the Instant Pot. Pour a cup of water.
2. Cut a large parchment paper and place the fish in the middle.3. Pour over the green chutney.
3. Fold and secure the parchment paper.
4. Place on top of the steamer basket.
5. Close the lid and press the Manual button.
6. Adjust the cooking time to 10 minutes.
7. Do natural pressure release.

Szechuan Shrimps

Serves: 4 | Cooking Time: 6 Minutes

Ingredients:

- 1 tbsp. julienned ginger
- 1½ lbs. unpeeled raw shrimps
- 3 tbsps. soy sauce
- 2 tbsps. crushed red pepper
- Salt and pepper, to taste
- 3 tbsps. chopped green scallions

Directions:

1. Place all ingredients in the Instant Pot.
2. Lock the lid. Select the Manual mode and cook for 6 minutes at Low Pressure.
3. Once cooking is complete, do a quick pressure release. Carefully open the lid.
4. Garnish with green scallions and serve.

White Wine Squid With Green Beans

Serves:4 | Cooking Time: 45 Minutes

Ingredients:

- 1 lb squid, chopped
- 1 lb green beans
- 1 green onion, chopped
- 2 cups canned tomatoes
- 1 tbsp white wine
- Salt and black pepper to taste

Directions:

1. Coat the pressure cooker with cooking spray and cook the onion for 3 minutes until soft. Add squid and cook for another 3 minutes, stirring occasionally. Add in the remaining ingredients, and give it a good stir. Add water, enough to cover everything, and seal lid. Cook on Manual at High for 20 minutes. Once ready, do a natural pressure release for 10 minutes. Serve.

Omato Clam & Shrimps

Serves: 2 | Cooking Time: 15 Minutes

Ingredients:

- 4 cups Tomato Clam Cocktail1 chopped onion2 tablespoons butter
- 1 teaspoon dried oregano1 tablespoon smoked paprika½ teaspoon salt
- ½ cup grated Parmesan cheese
- ½ teaspoon ground black pepper1 ½ cup Arborio rice1 cup shrimp, deveined

Directions:

1. Select the "Sauté" function on your Instant pot then add the oil to its insert.
2. Add the onions to the heated oil, cook for 3 minutes then add all the seasoning.
3. Cook for another 2 minutes then add the rice to the pot.
4. Pour in Tomato Clam Cocktail to the rice then cover the lid.
5. Secure the cooker lid and set it on the "Manual" settings at high pressure for 10 minutes.
6. After the beep, do a Quick release then remove the lid.
7. Stir in shrimp to the rice soup. Cover the lid and let it stay for 5 minutes.
8. Drizzled grated parmesan cheese on top then serve.

Beef & Lamb , pork Recipes

Beef & Lamb , pork Recipes

Simple Shredded Beef

Serves: 4-6 | Cooking Time: 1 Hour 20 Minutes

Ingredients:

- 3½ lbs beef chuck roast
- 2 tbsp olive oil
- 1 tsp sea salt
- 2½ cups beef broth

Directions:

1. Preheat the Instant Pot by selecting SAUTÉ. Add the oil.
2. Season the meat with salt.
3. Add the beef roast to the pot and sauté for 8-10 minutes on both sides, until browned.
4. Close and lock the lid. Press the CANCEL button to reset the cooking program, then select the MANUAL setting and set the cooking time for 75 minutes at HIGH pressure.
5. Once cooking is complete, select CANCEL and let Naturally Release for 10 minutes. Release any remaining steam manually. Uncover the pot.
6. Remove the beef roast from the pot and shred the meat with 2 forks.
7. Return to the Instant Pot and stir with remaining liquid.
8. Serve with cooked rice, potato or pasta. Also you can use the meat in sandwiches, burrito bowls, tacos, and more.

Green Onion Pork Frittata

Serves: 2-4 | Cooking Time: 30 Minutes

Ingredients:

- 1 tbsp butter, melted
- 1 cup green onions, chopped
- 1 pound ground pork, chopped
- 6 eggs
- Salt and black pepper, to taste
- 1 cup water

Directions:

1. In a deep bowl, break the eggs and whisk until frothy. Mix in the onions and ground meat, and season with the salt and pepper. Grease a casserole dish with 1 tablespoon of melted butter. Pour the egg mixture into the dish.
2. Place a metal trivet in the pressure cooker and add 1 cup of water. Select Rice mode and cook for 25 minutes on High. Do a quick pressure release and serve immediately.

Cumin Pork Chops With Peach Sauce

Serves: 4 | Cooking Time: 20 Minutes

Ingredients:

- 4 pork chops
- 1 tsp cumin seeds
- Salt and black pepper to taste
- 2 cups peaches, sliced
- 1 tbsp vegetable oil
- ¾ cup vegetable stock

Directions:

1. Sprinkle salt, cumin, and black pepper on the pork chops. Set on Sauté and warm oil. Add the chops and cook for 3 to 5 minutes until browned and set aside on a bowl.
2. Arrange peach slices at the bottom of the cooker. Place the pork chops on top of the plumes. Add any juice from the plate over the pork and apply stock around the edges.
3. Seal lid and cook on High Pressure for 8 minutes. Do a quick Pressure release. Transfer the pork chops to a serving plate and spoon over the peach sauce before serving.

Garlic Beef Sirloin

Serves: 8 | Cooking Time: 35 Minutes

Ingredients:

- 6 lbs beef top sirloin steak
- 4 teaspoons garlic powder
- 8 cloves garlic, minced
- 1 cup butter
- Salt and pepper to taste

Directions:

1. Select the 'sauté' function on the instant pot.
2. Add the butter to the pot and add the sirloin steaks. Cook for 5 minutes. Let the meat brown on each side.

3. Stir in all the remaining ingredients and secure the lid.
4. Switch the cooker to the 'meat stew' mode and cook for 30 minutes.
5. After the beep, 'natural release' the steam and remove the lid.
6. Serve hot.

Lemon Beef Meal

Serves: 2 | Cooking Time: 10 Minutes

Ingredients:

- 1 tbsp. olive oil
- 2 beef steaks
- ½ tsp. garlic salt
- 1 garlic clove, crushed
- 2 tbsps. lemon juice

Directions:

1. Press Sauté on the Instant Pot. Heat the olive oil in the pot until shimmering.
2. Add the beef and garlic salt and sauté for 4 to 5 minutes to evenly brown.
3. Add the garlic and sauté for 1 minute until fragrant.
4. Serve with lemon juice on top.

Beer Pork Roast With Mushrooms

Serves: 8 | Cooking Time: 50 Minutes

Ingredients:

- 3 pounds pork roast
- 8 ounces mushrooms, sliced
- 12 ounces root beer
- 10 ounces cream mushroom soup
- 1 package dry onion soup

Directions:

1. In the pressure cooker, whisk together mushroom soup, dry onion soup mix, and root beer. Add the mushrooms and pork.
2. Seal the lid, and set to Meat/Stew mode for 40 minutes on High. When ready, let sit for 5 minutes before doing a quick pressure release.

Party Apple-glazed Pork Ribs

Serves: 4 | Cooking Time: 45 Minutes

Ingredients:

- ½ cup apple cider vinegar
- 2 pounds pork ribs
- 3 ½ cups apple juice
- Salt and black pepper to taste

Directions:

1. Pour apple juice and apple cider vinegar into the pressure cooker and lower the trivet. Season the pork ribs with salt and pepper, and place on top of the trivet and seal the lid. Cook on High pressure for 30 minutes. Once it goes off, let the valve drop on its own for a natural release, for about 10 minutes.

Indian Roasted Pork

Serves: 3 | Cooking Time: 8 Hours

Ingredients:

- 1 tbsp. olive oil
- 1 lb. pork loin
- 1 tsp. cumin
- 2 garlic cloves, roughly chopped
- 1 onion, sliced
- Salt and pepper, to taste

Directions:

1. Coat the Instant Pot with olive oil and add the pork loin. Set aside.
2. In a food processor, place the remaining ingredients.
3. Pulse until smooth then pour the mixture over the pork loin.
4. Lock the lid. Press the Slow Cook button and set the cooking time to 8 hours at High Pressure.
5. Once cooking is complete, perform a natural pressure release for 10 minutes, and then release any remaining pressure. Carefully open the lid.
6. Allow to cool for a few minutes. Remove them from the pot and serve warm.

Pork Tenderloin With Pepper Jelly Glaze

Servings:4 | Cooking Time: 35 Minutes

Ingredients:

- ½ cup apple juice
- ½ cup hot pepper jelly
- 2 tablespoons apple cider vinegar
- 1 large pork tenderloin
- 1 teaspoon kosher salt
- Freshly ground black pepper
- ¼ cup water
- 1½ teaspoons cornstarch

Directions:

1. In the inner pot, whisk together the apple juice, hot pepper jelly, and vinegar until smooth.
2. Season the pork with the salt and pepper and add it to the pot (cut the tenderloin in half if necessary to fit in the pot). Pour in the water.
3. Lock the lid into place. Select Pressure Cook or Manual; set the pressure to High and the time to 5 minutes.
4. After the cook time is complete, let the pressure release Naturally for 5 minutes, then Quick release any remaining pressure. Unlock and remove the lid. Transfer the pork to a cutting board.
5. Select Sauté and set the heat to Medium. Add the cornstarch and whisk until the sauce thickens, about 5 minutes.
6. Slice the pork and serve with the sauce on top.

Pineapple & Soda-glazed Ham

Serves:6 | Cooking Time: 33 Minutes

Ingredients:

- 4 lb picnic ham
- 1 can cola-flavored soda
- 1 (15 ¼-oz) can pineapple rings with juice

Directions:

1. Add the ham to the IP with the fattier side facing downwards. Place the pineapple rings over the ham, attach them with toothpicks. Pour soda and pineapple juice, all over the ham. Seal the lid, select Manual at High, and cook for 8 minutes. When ready, release the pressure naturally for 5 minutes. Serve hot or cold.

Barbecued Pork Ribs

Servings:x | Cooking Time: 45 Minutes

Ingredients:

- 1 pound country style pork ribs
- Coarse sea salt and freshly ground black pepper, to taste
- 1/2 teaspoon red pepper flakes
- 1/4 cup Marsala wine
- 1/4 cup chicken broth
- 1/2 cup BBQ sauce

Directions:

1. Place the pork ribs, salt, black pepper, red pepper, wine, and chicken broth in the inner pot.
2. Choose the "Meat/Stew" mode and cook for 35 minutes at High pressure. Once cooking is complete, use a quick pressure release; carefully remove the lid.
3. Transfer the pork ribs to a baking pan. Pour the BBQ sauce over the pork ribs and roast in the preheated oven at 425 °F for 6 to 8 minutes. Bon appétit!

Western Shoulder Ribs

Serves: 8 | Cooking Time: 40 Minutes

Ingredients:

- 3 pounds pork shoulder
- 2 teaspoons salt
- 1 teaspoon barbecue rub
- ½ cup water
- ½ cup commercial barbecue sauce

Directions:

1. Place all ingredients in the Instant Pot.
2. Close the lid and press the Meat/Stew button.
3. Adjust the cooking time to 40 minutes.
4. Do natural pressure release.

Bbq Pulled Pork

Serves: 9 | Cooking Time: 60 Minutes

Ingredients:

- ½ cup BBQ sauce
- ½ cup chicken broth
- 3 pounds pork roast
- Salt and pepper

Directions:

1. Place all ingredients in the Instant Pot.
2. Close the lid and press the Meat/Stew button.

3. Adjust the cooking time to 60 minutes.
4. Do natural pressure release.
5. Once the lid is open, take the pork out and use two forks to shred the meat.
6. Serve with the sauce.

Sticky Barbecue Pork Ribs

Servings: 4 | Cooking Time: 60 Minutes

Ingredients:

- 1 rack pork baby back ribs
- 1 tbsp garlic powder
- 1 tsp New Mexico chili powder
- 1 tsp mustard powder
- 4 tbsp BBQ sauce
- Salt and black pepper to taste

Directions:

1. Rub the back ribs with garlic powder, chili, mustard, salt, and pepper. Pour 1 cup of water into the pot and fit in a trivet. Place the ribs on the trivet. Seal the lid, select Pressure Cook on High, and set the time to 25 minutes.
2. When done cooking, allow a natural release for 10 minutes. Unlock the lid and remove the ribs to a lined baking sheet.
3. Brush with BBQ sauce and set under the broiler for 10-15 minutes until the ribs are sticky and charred. Serve warm.

Frittata With Shallots And Ground Pork

Serves:5 | Cooking Time: 30 Minutes

Ingredients:

- 1 tbsp butter, melted
- 2 cups shallots, chopped
- ½ lb ground pork, cooked
- 1 tsp sage
- 6 eggs
- Salt and black pepper to taste

Directions:

1. In a deep bowl, break the eggs and whisk until frothy. Mix in shallots and ground pork, sage, and season with salt and pepper. Grease a casserole dish with butter and pour in the egg mixture. Place a trivet in the pressure cooker and add 1 cup of water. Place the dish on top and seal the lid. Select Manual and cook for 25 minutes at High. Do a quick pressure release and serve.

Bacon With Braised Red Cabbage

Serves: 2 | Cooking Time: 20 Minutes

Ingredients:

- ¼ pound red cabbage, chopped
- 2 bacon slices, chopped
- ½ cup beef broth
- ½ tbsp butter
- Salt and black pepper to taste

Directions:

1. Add the bacon slices in IP, and cook for 5 minutes, until crispy, on Sauté. Stir in cabbage, salt, pepper, and butter. Seal the lid, select Steam mode for 10 minutes on High. When ready, release the pressure naturally, for 10 minutes.

Instant Pot Nikujaga

Serves: 4 | Cooking Time: 45 Minutes

Ingredients:

- 10 green beans, trimmed
- 1 onion, chopped
- 1 carrots, cubed
- 2 potatoes, cubed
- ½ pounds sliced beef chuck Salt

Directions:

1. Place all ingredients in the Instant Pot.
2. Close the lid and press the Meat/Stew button.
3. Adjust the cooking time to 45 minutes.
4. Do natural pressure release.

Chimichurri Beef Tips

Servings:6 | Cooking Time: 35 Minutes

Ingredients:

- 1 tablespoon extra-virgin olive oil
- 1½ pounds stewing beef, cut into ½-inch-wide strips
- ½ onion, chopped
- ¼ cup water
- ½ cup chimichurri

Directions:

1. Select Sauté, set the heat to Medium, and add the olive oil. When it shimmers, add the beef and onion and sauté for about 2 minutes to brown the beef and soften the onion. There is no need to cook the meat all

the way through.

2. Add the water and chimichurri.

3. Lock the lid into place. Select Pressure Cook or Manual; set the pressure to High and the time to 10 minutes.

4. After the cook time is complete, let the pressure release Naturally. Unlock and remove the lid. Transfer the beef and sauce to a serving dish and serve.

Pork Vindaloo (curry Pork)

Serves: 6 | Cooking Time: 35 Minutes

Ingredients:

- ¼ cup coconut oil
- 2 lbs. pork shoulder, sliced
- 1 tbsp. garam masala
- 3 tbsps. freshly squeezed lemon juice
- 1 cup water
- Salt and pepper, to taste

Directions:

1. Press the Sauté button on the Instant Pot and heat the coconut oil until melted.

2. Add and sear the pork loin on all sides for 3 minutes or until lightly browned.

3. Add the garam masala and continue sauté for 2 more minutes.

4. Stir in the lemon juice and water. Sprinkle with salt and pepper.

5. Lock the lid. Press the Meat/Stew button and set the cooking time to 30 minutes at High Pressure.

6. Once cooking is complete, perform a natural pressure release for 10 minutes, and then release any remaining pressure. Carefully open the lid.

7. Remove the pork from the pot and serve warm.

Pork Carnitas

Servings:8 | Cooking Time: 1 Hour

Ingredients:

- 2 tablespoons vegetable oil
- 2¼ pounds pork shoulder roast or Boston butt, cut into 2-inch pieces
- 1 teaspoon kosher salt
- 1 teaspoon ground cumin
- ½ teaspoon freshly ground black pepper
- 1 cup freshly squeezed orange juice
- ¼ cup freshly squeezed lime juice
- 2 bay leaves

Directions:

1. Select Sauté and set the heat to High. Heat the oil in the pot until it shimmers. Add the pork and fry for 6 to 8 minutes, until light golden brown. Season with the salt, cumin, and pepper. Add the orange and lime juices and top with the bay leaves.

2. Lock the lid into place. Select Pressure Cook or Manual; set the pressure to High and the time to 25 minutes.

3. After the cook time is complete, let the pressure release Naturally. Unlock and remove the lid. Remove and discard the bay leaves. Using two forks, shred the carnitas in the pot.

Bacon & Potato Brussels Sprouts

Serves: 4 | Cooking Time: 20 Minutes

Ingredients:

- 4 bacon slices, chopped
- 1 lb Brussels sprouts, halved
- 1 cup potatoes, cubed
- ½ cup chicken stock
- Salt and black pepper to taste

Directions:

1. Set to Sauté your Instant Pot and add the bacon. Cook for 5-6 minutes until crispy; remove to a paper-lined plate. Add potatoes, Brussels sprouts, chicken stock, salt, and pepper the pot. Seal the lid, select Manual, and cook for 5 minutes on High pressure. When done, perform a quick pressure release.Top with bacon. Serve warm.

Parmesan Pork Chops

Serves: 4 | Cooking Time: 20 Minutes

Ingredients:

- 1 tablespoon lard, at room temperature
- 4 pork chops, bone-in
- Sea salt and freshly ground black pepper, to taste
- 1/4 cup tomato puree
- 1 cup chicken bone broth
- 4 ounces parmesan cheese, preferably freshly grated

Directions:

1. Press the "Sauté" button and melt the lard. Sear the pork chops for 3 to 4 minutes per side. Season with salt and pepper.

2. Place the tomato puree and chicken broth in the inner pot.

3. Secure the lid. Choose the "Manual" mode and cook for 10 minutes at High pressure. Once cooking is complete, use a natural pressure release; carefully remove the lid.

4. Top with parmesan cheese and serve warm. Bon appétit!

Simple Roast Lamb

Serves: 4 | Cooking Time: 40 Minutes

Ingredients:

- 2 lb lamb leg
- 1 tbsp garlic powder
- 3 tbsp extra virgin olive oil
- Salt and black pepper to taste
- 4 rosemary sprigs, chopped

Directions:

1. Grease the inner pot with oil. Rub the meat with salt, pepper, and garlic powder, and place in the instant pot. Pour enough water to cover and seal the lid. Cook on Meat/Stew for 30 minutes on High. Do a quick release. Make sure the meat is tender and falls off the bones. Top with cooking juices and rosemary.

Plum Sauce Pork Chops

Serves: 2-4 | Cooking Time: 20 Minutes

Ingredients:

- 4 pork chops
- 1 tsp cumin seeds
- Salt and black pepper to taste
- 2 cups firm plums, pitted and chopped
- 1 tbsp vegetable oil
- ¾ cup vegetable stock

Directions:

1. Sprinkle salt, cumin, and pepper on the pork chops. Set on Sauté and warm oil. Add the chops and cook for 3 to 5 minutes and set aside on a bowl. Arrange plum slices at the bottom of the cooker. Place pork chops on top of the plumes. Add any juice from the plate over the pork and apply stock around the edges. Seal lid and cook on High for 8 minutes. Do a quick Pressure release. Transfer pork chops to a serving plate and spoon over the plum sauce.

Italian Pork Cutlets

Serves: 6 | Cooking Time: 20 Minutes

Ingredients:

- 4 tbsps. olive oil
- 6 pork cutlets
- Salt and pepper, to taste
- 1 tbsp. Italian herb mix
- 1½ cups water

Directions:

1. In the Instant Pot, add all the ingredients. Stir to combine well.

2. Lock the lid. Press the Meat/Stew button and set the cooking time to 20 minutes at High Pressure.

3. Once cooking is complete, do a natural pressure release for 10 minutes, and then release any remaining pressure. Carefully open the lid.

4. Remove the meat and serve immediately.

Beer-braised Pulled Ham

Serves: 16 | Cooking Time: 60 Minutes

Ingredients:

- 2 bottles of beer
- ¾ cup Dijon mustard
- ½ teaspoon ground black pepper
- 1 bone-in ham
- 4 sprigs of rosemary

Directions:

1. Place all ingredients in the Instant Pot.
2. Close the lid and press the Meat/Stew button.
3. Adjust the cooking time to 60 minutes.
4. Do natural pressure release.
5. Take the pork out and use two forks to shred the meat.

Fried Rice With Sausage And Egg

Serves: 2 | Cooking Time: 15 Minutes

Ingredients:

- 1 tsp. butter
- 2 oz. chorizo sausage, thinly sliced
- 2 large eggs, beaten
- 2 cups cooked rice
- 1 red bell pepper, chopped
- Salt and pepper, to taste

Directions:

1. Press Sauté on the Instant Pot. Heat the butter in the pot until melted.
2. Add the sausage and sauté for 2 to 3 minutes per side to evenly brown.
3. Add the beaten eggs and sauté for 2 to 3 minutes to scramble.
4. Add the rice and bell pepper. Sprinkle with salt and pepper. Sauté for 5 minutes; serve warm.

Easy Bbq Pulled Pork

Serves: 4-6 | Cooking Time: 1 Hour 25 Minutes

Ingredients:
- 3 lbs pork roast, cut into 4 chunks
- ½ tsp kosher salt
- ½ tsp ground black pepper
- 2/3 cup chicken broth
- ½ cup BBQ sauce

Directions:
1. Rub all sides of the pork roast with salt and pepper.
2. Put the meat in the Instant Pot.
3. Pour in the broth and BBQ sauce, stir.
4. Close and lock the lid. Select MANUAL and cook at HIGH pressure for 60 minutes.
5. Once cooking is complete, select Cancel and let Naturally Release for 10 minutes. Release any remaining steam manually. Uncover the pot.
6. Shred the meat with two forks.
7. Serve with the gravy.

Smoked Pull Pork

Serves: 12 | Cooking Time: 60 Minutes

Ingredients:
- 3 ½ pounds pork butt roast
- 1 cup chicken broth
- 2 tablespoons soy sauce
- 2 tablespoons liquid smoke
- 2 cloves of garlic, minced

Directions:
1. Place all ingredients in the Instant Pot.
2. Close the lid and press the Meat/Stew button.
3. Adjust the cooking time to 60 minutes.
4. Do natural pressure release.
5. Once the lid is open, take the pork out and use two forks to shred the meat.
6. Serve with the sauce.

Teriyaki Pork Tenderloin

Serves: 4 | Cooking Time: 45 Minutes

Ingredients:
- 2 pork tenderloins (1 lb each), cut into half
- 2 tbsp olive oil
- Salt and ground black pepper to taste
- 2 cups teriyaki sauce
- Sesame seeds, toasted
- 4 green onions, chopped

Directions:
1. Set your instant pot on SAUTÉ mode, add the oil and heat it up.
2. Rub all sides of the tenderloins with salt and pepper.
3. Add the tenderloins and cook for few minutes until lightly brown on both sides. You may have to do it in two batches.
4. Pour the teriyaki sauce over the meat. Close and lock the lid.
5. Press the CANCEL button to reset the cooking program, then select the MANUAL setting and set the cooking time for 20 minutes at HIGH pressure.
6. Once cooking is complete, select CANCEL and let Naturally Release for 10 minutes. Release any remaining steam manually. Uncover the pot.
7. Slice the meat, top with toasted sesame seeds and green onions, serve.

Smokey And Spicy Pork Roast

Serves: 12 | Cooking Time: 1 Hour

Ingredients:
- 1 tbsp. cayenne pepper flakes
- 5 tbsps. olive oil
- Salt and pepper, to taste
- 2 tbsps. liquid smoke
- 4 lbs. pork butt
- 1 cup water

Directions:
1. Place all ingredients in the Instant Pot. Stir to combine well.
2. Lock the lid. Press the Meat/Stew button and set the cooking time to 1 hour at High Pressure.
3. Once cooking is complete, perform a natural pressure release for 10 to 20 minutes, and then release any remaining pressure. Carefully open the lid.
4. Remove the pork from the pot and serve warm.

Paprika Pork Loin Roast

Serves: 9 | Cooking Time: 50 Minutes

Ingredients:

- 4 tbsps. olive oil
- 4 garlic cloves
- ½ cup chopped paprika
- 3 lbs. pork loin roast
- Salt and pepper, to taste
- 1 cup water

Directions:

1. Press the Sauté button on the Instant Pot. Coat the pot with olive oil.
2. Add and sauté the garlic and paprika for 1 minute or until fragrant.
3. Add the pork loin roast and sear on all sides for 3 minutes or until lightly browned.
4. Sprinkle salt and pepper for seasoning. Pour in the water.
5. Lock the lid. Press the Meat/Stew button and set the cooking time to 45 minutes at High Pressure.
6. Once cooking is complete, perform a natural pressure release for 10 minutes, and then release any remaining pressure. Carefully open the lid.
7. Allow to cool for a few minutes. Remove the pork from the pot and baste with the juice remains in the pot before serving.

Beef Tenderloin With Cauliflower

Serves: 4 | Cooking Time: 25 Minutes

Ingredients:

- 1½ lbs. beef tenderloin
- 1 tsp. sea salt
- 1 tbsp. extra virgin olive oil
- 4 garlic cloves, finely chopped
- 4 cups cauliflower florets

Directions:

1. On a clean work surface, slice the beef tenderloin into 1-inch thick slices and rub with salt.
2. Put the olive oil in the Instant Pot, set the Sauté setting.
3. Add and brown the beef for 4 to 5 minutes, then add the garlic and sauté for a minute.
4. Add the cauliflower.
5. Lock the lid. Set the Instant Pot to Manual mode and set the cooking time for 20 minutes at High Pressure.

6. Once cooking is complete, use a quick pressure release.
7. Carefully open the lid. Allow to cool for a few minutes. Transfer them on a large plate and serve immediately.

Bbq Beef Ribs

Serves: 7 | Cooking Time: 60 Minutes

Ingredients:

- 3 pounds beef ribs
- Salt and pepper
- 2 cups BBQ sauce
- 2 tablespoons pepper jelly
- ½ cup beef broth

Directions:

1. Season the ribs with salt and pepper.
2. Place in the Instant Pot and pour over the rest of the ingredients.
3. Close the lid and press the Meat/Stew button.
4. Adjust the cooking time to 60 minutes.
5. Do natural pressure release.

Steamed Red Cabbage With Crispy Bacon

Serves: 8 | Cooking Time: 25 Minutes

Ingredients:

- 1 pound red cabbage, chopped
- 8 bacon slices, chopped
- 1 ½ cups beef broth
- 2 tbsp butter
- Salt and black pepper to taste

Directions:

1. Add the bacon slices in your pressure cooker, and cook for 5 minutes, until crispy, on Sauté. Stir in the cabbage, broth, salt, pepper, and butter. Seal the lid, select Steam mode for 10 minutes on High pressure. When ready, release the pressure naturally, for 10 minutes.

Pork Chops In Cream Of Mushrooms

Serves:4 | Cooking Time: 35 Minutes

Ingredients:

- 10 oz condensed cream of mushroom soup
- Salt and black pepper to taste
- 1 cup milk
- 4 boneless pork chops
- 1 tbsp ranch dressing

Directions:

1. Combine all the ingredients, except for the pork chops, in a mixing bowl. Place the chops into the IP, and pour mixture over. Pour in ½ cup of water. Seal the lid, select Manual at High, and cook for 10 minutes. When ready, release the pressure naturally for 10 minutes.

Pork Chops Teriyaki Style

Serves:4 | Cooking Time: 35 Minutes

Ingredients:

- 1/3 cup Teriyaki sauce
- 1 tbsp brown sugar
- 4 boneless pork chops
- ½ tsp fresh ginger, minced

Directions:

1. Except for pork chops, mix all ingredients with 1 cup water in a mixing bowl. Place pork chops into the IP, and pour mixture over pork chops. Seal the lid, select Manual at High, and cook for 12 minutes. When ready, release the pressure naturally for 5 minutes. Serve hot.

Picante Lamb Chops

Serves: 6 | Cooking Time: 35 Minutes

Ingredients:

- 6 lamb chops, bone-in
- 1¼ apples, peeled and sliced
- 1¼ cup Picante sauce3 tablespoons olive oil
- 3 tablespoons all-purpose flour
- 3 tablespoons brown sugar, packed

Directions:

1. Dredge the lamb chops through a bowl of flour.
2. Mix the apple slices, picante sauce and brown sugar in a bowl.

3. Pour the oil into the instant pot and select 'sauté'.
4. Add the flour covered chops to the oil and sear for 5 minutes.
5. Secure the lid and select the 'meat stew" function. Cook for 35 minutes at high pressure.
6. Once done 'Natural release' the steam for 10 minutes, then remove the lid.
7. Serve warm.

Pork Chops And Potatoes And Onion

Servings:x | Cooking Time: 20 Minutes

Ingredients:

- 1 tablespoon lard, at room temperature
- 2 pork chops
- 1 cup chicken broth
- 1/2 onion, sliced
- 1/2 pound potatoes, quartered
- Sea salt and ground black pepper, to taste

Directions:

1. Press the "Sauté" button and melt the lard. Once hot, brown the pork chops for 3 minutes per side.
2. Add the remaining ingredients.
3. Secure the lid. Choose the "Manual" mode and cook for 10 minutes at High pressure. Once cooking is complete, use a natural pressure release; carefully remove the lid.
4. Serve warm.

Bell Pepper And Beef

Serves: 4 | Cooking Time: 30 Minutes

Ingredients:

- 1½ lbs. beef tenderloin
- 1 tsp. sea salt
- 4 green bell peppers, deseeded and stems removed
- 1 tbsp. extra virgin olive oil
- 1 red onion, peeled and diced
- 1 cup water

Directions:

1. On a clean work surface, cut the beef into 1-inch thick slices, sprinkle with salt
2. Cut the bell peppers into ¼-inch slices.
3. Set Instant Pot to Sauté setting, then add extra virgin olive oil and heat until hot.
4. Add the beef and cook for 4 to 5 minutes or until browned.

5. Add peppers and onion, and sauté for 2 minutes. Pour in the water.
6. Lock the lid. Set the Instant Pot to the Manual setting and set the timer at 30 minutes at High Pressure.
7. When the timer beeps, press Cancel, then use a quick pressure release.
8. Carefully open the lid and allow to cool for a few minutes. Serve warm.

Pork Loin With Mustard Sauce

Serves:6 | Cooking Time: 68 Minutes

Ingredients:

- 3 lb boneless pork loin roast
- 2 tbsp olive oil
- 1 cup chicken broth
- 2 cups onions, chopped
- Mustard sauce to taste
- 2 tsp paprika
- Salt and black pepper to taste

Directions:

1. Set your IP to Sauté and heat olive oil. Add the onions and cook for 3 minutes. Pour in the broth. Sprinkle pork with salt, pepper, and paprika. Place the roast into the IP, seal the lid, select Manual at High, and cook for 45 minutes. When ready, release the pressure naturally for 10 minutes. Remove the pork and let it rest for 10 minutes before slicing, covered with foil. Strain the onions and sprinkle around the pork. Serve with mustard sauce.

Pork Rib Chops With Carrots & Parsnips

Serves:4 | Cooking Time: 35 Minutes

Ingredients:

- 4 pork rib chops
- 1 cup carrots, thinly sliced
- 1 cup parsnips, thinly sliced
- 1 onion, sliced into rings
- 1 ½ cups bbq sauce
- Salt and black pepper to taste

Directions:

1. Add the pork chops in your IP. In a bowl, combine bbq sauce, 2 cups of water, onions, parsnips, and carrots, and stir. Pour over the pork. Seal the lid, select Manual, and cook for 20 minutes at High. Once ready, release the pressure quickly. Open the lid, drizzle with the remaining bbq sauce and serve.

Basic Pork Chops

Serves: 6 | Cooking Time: 30 Minutes

Ingredients:

- 3 tbsps. butter
- 3 garlic cloves, minced
- 6 boneless pork chops
- ½ cup heavy cream
- ½ cup chicken broth
- Salt and pepper, to taste

Directions:

1. Press the Sauté button on the Instant Pot.
2. Heat the butter until melted and add and sauté the garlic for 1 minute or until fragrant.
3. Add the pork chops and sear for 3 minutes on each side until lightly browned.
4. Add the heavy cream and broth. Sprinkle salt and pepper for seasoning.
5. Lock the lid. Press the Meat/Stew button and set the cooking time to 30 minutes at High Pressure.
6. Once cooking is complete, perform a natural pressure release for 10 minutes, and then release any remaining pressure. Carefully open the lid.
7. Allow to cool for a few minutes. Remove the pork from the pot and baste with the juice remains in the pot before serving.

Ranch Potatoes With Ham

Serves: 4 | Cooking Time: 20 Minutes

Ingredients:

- 1 lb Yukon gold potatoes, quartered
- 4 oz cooked ham, chopped
- 1 tsp garlic powder
- 2 tsp chives, chopped
- Salt to taste
- 1/3 cup Ranch dressing

Directions:

1. Cover potatoes with salted water in your Instant Pot and seal the lid. Select Manual and cook for 7 minutes on High pressure. When done, perform a quick pressure release and unlock the lid. Drain the potatoes and transfer to a bowl. Stir in ranch dressing, garlic powder, and ham. Sprinkle with chives and serve.

Coconut Pork

Serves: 4 | Cooking Time: 25 Minutes

Ingredients:

- 1 tbsp. extra virgin olive oil
- 4 pork chops
- 1 tbsp. grated ginger
- 1 tsp. sea salt
- 2 cups coconut milk

Directions:

1. Lightly coat the Instant Pot with olive oil and select the setting to Sauté.
2. Add and brown the pork chops for 3 minutes.
3. Add the remaining ingredients to the pot. Stir to combine well.
4. Lock the lid. Set the Manual mode and set the cooking time to 25 minutes at High Pressure.
5. Once cooking is complete, use a natural pressure release for 10 minutes, then release any remaining pressure.
6. Carefully open the lid. Allow to cool for a few minutes. Transfer them on a large plate and serve immediately.

Salsa-braised Pork

Servings:6 | Cooking Time: 50 Minutes

Ingredients:

- 1 packet taco seasoning
- 2 pounds boneless pork loin roast
- 1 tablespoon vegetable oil
- 2½ cups Garden Salsa or store-bought salsa

Directions:

1. Sprinkle the taco seasoning on all sides of the pork loin.
2. Select Sauté, set the heat to Medium, and add the oil. When it shimmers, add the pork, fat side down, and cook undisturbed for 3 to 4 minutes, until golden brown. Turn and sear the other side for 3 to 4 minutes. Add the salsa.
3. Lock the lid into place. Select Pressure Cook or Manual; set the pressure to High and the time to 10 minutes.
4. After the cook time is complete, let the pressure release Naturally for 10 minutes, then Quick release any remaining pressure. Unlock and remove the lid. Remove the pork from the sauce and let cool for a couple of minutes before slicing.

5. Cut the meat across the grain into slices about ½ inch thick. It's okay if it is not quite done in the center.
6. Select Sauté, set the heat to Low, and bring the sauce to a simmer. Place any underdone center slices in the sauce and heat for several minutes until cooked through. Add the outer slices just to heat through. Serve with the sauce spooned over the top.

Spring Onion & Ground Pork Egg Casserole

Serves: 5 | Cooking Time: 30 Minutes

Ingredients:

- 1 tbsp butter, melted
- 1 cup spring onions, chopped
- 1 pound ground pork, chopped
- 6 eggs
- Salt and black pepper, to taste
- 1 cup water

Directions:

1. In a bowl, break the eggs and whisk until frothy. Mix in the onions and ground meat, and season with the salt and pepper. Grease a casserole dish with 1 tablespoon of melted butter. Pour the egg mixture into the dish.
2. Place a metal trivet in the pressure cooker and add 1 cup of water. Select RICE mode and cook for 25 minutes on High. Do a quick pressure release and serve immediately.

Short Ribs With Butter And Olive Salad

Servings:4 | Cooking Time: 55 Minutes

Ingredients:

- 4 pounds bone-in beef short ribs
- 2 teaspoons kosher salt
- Freshly ground black pepper
- 2 tablespoons unsalted butter
- 1 small onion, chopped
- 2 garlic cloves, minced
- ⅓ cup water
- ½ cup Italian or New Orleans–style olive salad

Directions:

1. Season the ribs with the salt and pepper.
2. Select Sauté, set the heat to Medium, and add the butter. When it foams, add the onion and garlic to the

pot and cook for about 2 minutes, or until the onion is translucent. Add the ribs and brown them on each side, about 5 minutes in total.

3. Add the water and olive salad.

4. Lock the lid into place. Select Pressure Cook or Manual; set the pressure to High and the time to 30 minutes.

5. After the cook time is complete, let the pressure release Naturally. Unlock and remove the lid. Transfer the ribs to a serving dish. Top them with the olive sauce from the pot and serve.

Big Papa's Roast

Serves: 6 | Cooking Time: 1 Hour

Ingredients:

- 3 lbs. beef chuck roast
- 2 tsps. salt
- 6 peppercorns, crushed
- 2 tbsps. extra virgin olive oil
- 2 cups beef stock

Directions:

1. On a clean work surface, rub the beef with salt and peppercorns.

2. Coat the Instant Pot with olive oil and set the Sauté setting. Heat the oil until shimmering.

3. Add and brown the beef roast for 4 to 5 minutes.

4. Pour in the beef stock.

5. Lock the lid. Set to Manual mode, set the cooking time for 60 minutes at High Pressure.

6. Once cooking is complete, use a natural pressure release for 10 minutes, then release any remaining pressure.

7. Carefully open the lid. Allow to cool for a few minutes. Transfer them on a large plate and serve immediately.

Saucy Red Chili Pork

Servings: 4 | Cooking Time: 35 Minutes

Ingredients:

- 1 lb pork loin
- ¼ cup red chili puree
- 1 cup chicken broth
- Salt and black pepper to taste
- 1 tsp dried rosemary

Directions:

1. In the inner pot of your Instant Pot, combine pork, red chili puree, broth, salt, pepper, and rosemary. Seal the lid, select Pressure Cook on High, and set the time to 15 minutes.

2. Once done, allow a natural release for 10 minutes. Shred pork with two forks, stir and adjust taste with salt and pepper. Serve with rice and bread dishes.

Vegetable & Veg-
etarian Recipes

Vegetable & Vegetarian Recipes

Gyeran-jjim (korean Egg Custard)

Servings: 2 | Cooking Time: 25 Minutes

Ingredients:

- 2 tbsp sesame oil
- 4 large eggs
- ¾ tsp fish sauce
- 2 chopped green onions

Directions:

1. Beat eggs in a bowl until very smooth. Mix in fish sauce, 1 green onion, and 1 cup of water. Pour mixture into a ramekin and cover with foil. Pour 1 cup of water into the pot and fit in a trivet. Put the ramekin on the trivet.

2. Seal the lid, select Pressure Cook on Low, and set to 7 minutes. After cooking, allow a natural release for 10 minutes. Unlock the lid, carefully remove ramekin, top with remaining green onion. Drizzle with sesame oil to serve.

Sweet Potato Mash With Tahini

Serves: 2-4 | Cooking Time: 25 Minutes

Ingredients:

- 1 cup water
- 2 lb sweet potatoes, peeled and cubed
- 2 tbsp tahini
- 1 tbsp sugar
- ¼ tsp ground nutmeg
- Chopped fresh chives, for garnish
- Sea salt to taste

Directions:

1. Into the cooker, add 1 cup cold water and insert a steamer basket. Add sweet potato cubes into the steamer basket. Seal the lid and cook for 8 minutes at High Pressure. Release the pressure quickly.

2. In a bowl, add cooked sweet potatoes and slightly mash. Using a hand mixer, whip in nutmeg, sugar, and tahini until the sweet potatoes attain desired consistency. Add salt to taste and top with chives to serve.

Coconut Curry Tofu

Servings:4 | Cooking Time: 15 Minutes

Ingredients:

- 1 can full-fat coconut milk
- ¼ cup red or green curry paste
- 2 teaspoons unrefined sugar or brown sugar
- ¼ teaspoon kosher salt, plus more as needed
- ¼ cup water
- 1 package firm or extra-firm tofu, pressed and cubed
- 2 cups chopped fresh spinach

Directions:

1. In the inner pot, stir together the coconut milk, curry paste, sugar, salt, and water to combine. Add the tofu.

2. Lock the lid into place. Select Pressure Cook or Manual; set the pressure to High and the time to 3 minutes.

3. After the cook time is complete, Quick release the pressure. Unlock and remove the lid.

4. Add the spinach and stir until wilted. Taste and season with more salt, if needed, then serve.

Vegan Pumpkin Stew

Serves: 4 | Cooking Time: 10 Minutes

Ingredients:

- 3 cups pumpkin, sliced
- 5 cups vegetable stock
- 1 large can diced tomatoes Salt and pepper to taste
- 3 cups of mixed greens

Directions:

1. Place all ingredients in the Instant Pot.
2. Stir the contents and close the lid.
3. Close the lid and press the Manual button.
4. Adjust the cooking time to 10 minutes.
5. Do quick pressure release.

Instant Pot Veggie Stew

Serves: 5 | Cooking Time: 10 Minutes

Ingredients:

- ½ cup chopped tomatoes
- 1 stalk celery, minced
- 2 zucchinis, chopped
- 1 lb. mushrooms, sliced
- 1 onion, chopped
- Salt and pepper, to taste

Directions:

1. Place all ingredients in the Instant Pot.
2. Pour in enough water until half of the vegetables are submerged.
3. Lock the lid. Set the Instant Pot to Manual mode, then set the timer for 10 minutes at High Pressure.
4. Once cooking is complete, do a quick pressure release. Carefully open the lid.
5. Serve warm.

Brussels Sprouts With Potatoes

Serves: 2-4 | Cooking Time: 20 Minutes

Ingredients:

- 1½ lbs Brussels sprouts
- 1 cup new potatoes cut into 1 inch cubes
- ½ cup chicken stock
- Salt and ground black pepper to taste
- 1½ tbsp butter
- 1½ tbsp bread crumbs

Directions:

1. Wash the Brussels sprouts and remove the outer leaves, then cut into halves.
2. In the Instant pot, combine the potatoes, sprouts, stock, salt and pepper. Stir well.
3. Select MANUAL and cook at HIGH pressure for 5 minutes.
4. When the timer goes off, use a Quick Release. Carefully open the lid.
5. Select the SAUTÉ setting, add the butter and bread crumbs to the pot. Mix well and serve.

Carrot And Sweet Potato Medley

Serves: 6-8 | Cooking Time: 20 Minutes

Ingredients:

- 2 tbsp extra-virgin olive oil
- 1 medium onion, chopped
- 2 lbs baby carrots, halved
- 2 lbs sweet potatoes, peeled and cubed
- 1 cup veggie broth
- Salt and ground black pepper to taste

Directions:

1. Select the SAUTÉ setting on the Instant Pot and heat the oil.
2. Add the onion and sauté for 5 minutes, until softened.
3. Add the carrots, sweet potatoes and broth.
4. Season with salt and pepper. Stir well. Close and lock the lid.
5. Press the CANCEL button to stop the SAUTE function, then select the MANUAL setting and set the cooking time for 8 minutes at HIGH pressure.
6. When the timer beeps, use a Quick Release. Carefully unlock the lid.
7. Serve.

Green Beans With Fresh Garlic

Serves:2 | Cooking Time: 20 Minutes

Ingredients:

- 1 lb green beans, chopped
- 2 tbsp olive oil
- 1 cup fresh garlic cloves, minced
- Salt and black pepper to taste
- ¼ cup pomegranate seeds

Directions:

1. Heat olive oil on Sauté and cook garlic and green beans for 5 minutes. Season with salt and pepper, and stir. Pour in 1 cup of water in the IP, seal the lid, press Manual, and cook for 5 minutes at High. After cooking, do a quick pressure release. Serve topped with pomegranate seeds.

Zucchini And Tomato

Serves: 1 | Cooking Time: 10 Minutes

Ingredients:

- ¼ cup crumbled feta cheese
- 1 cup vegetable broth
- Salt and pepper, to taste
- ½ cup fresh cherry tomatoes
- 1 fresh zucchini, chopped

Directions:

1. Combine all the listed ingredients in the pot.
2. Lock the lid. Set the Instant Pot to Manual mode, then set the timer for 10 minutes at High Pressure.
3. Once cooking is complete, do a quick pressure release. Carefully open the lid.
4. Serve the chunky soup warm.

Curried Lentils

Servings:4 | Cooking Time: 55 Minutes

Ingredients:

- 1 tablespoon coconut oil
- 2 tablespoons mild curry powder
- 1 teaspoon ground ginger
- 1 cup dried green or brown lentils
- 3 cups water
- 1 teaspoon freshly squeezed lime juice
- ½ teaspoon kosher salt
- Freshly ground black pepper

Directions:

1. Select Sauté, set the heat to Medium, and add the coconut oil. When it shimmers, add the curry powder and ginger and toss to toast for 1 minute. Add the lentils and toss with the spices. Add the water.
2. Lock the lid into place. Select Pressure Cook or Manual; set the pressure to High and the time to 20 minutes.
3. After the cook time is complete, let the pressure release Naturally. Unlock and remove the lid.
4. Stir in the lime juice and season with the salt and pepper, then serve.

Carrot Puree

Serves: 2-4 | Cooking Time: 25 Minutes

Ingredients:

- 1 cup water
- 1½ lbs carrots, peeled and sliced into 1 inch pieces
- 1 tbsp honey
- 1 tbsp soy butter, softened
- ½ tsp kosher salt
- Brown sugar, optional

Directions:

1. Prepare the Instant Pot by adding the water to the pot and placing a steamer basket in it.
2. Put the carrots in the basket. Close and lock the lid.
3. Select the MANUAL setting and set the cooking time for 4 minutes at HIGH pressure.
4. Once timer goes off, use a Quick Release. Carefully unlock the lid.
5. Using a potato masher or electric beater, slowly blend the carrots until smooth and creamy.
6. Add the honey and butter and stir well. Season with salt and stir.
7. If desired, add sugar to taste. Serve.

Buttery Beets

Serves: 4-6 | Cooking Time: 45 Minutes

Ingredients:

- 1 cup water
- 1¾ lbs medium beets, trimmed
- 2 tbsp butter, melted
- Salt and freshly ground black pepper to taste
- 2 tbsp fresh parsley, chopped

Directions:

1. Prepare the Instant Pot by adding the water to the pot and placing the steamer basket in it.
2. Place the beets in the basket. Close and lock the lid.
3. Select MANUAL and cook at HIGH pressure for 24 minutes.
4. When the timer goes off, use a Quick Release. Carefully open the lid.
5. Transfer the beets to a plate and let them cool.
6. Peel and into wedges the beets and put in the bowl.
7. Add the butter, salt and pepper. Gently stir to coat the beets with the butter.
8. Sprinkle with parsley and serve.

Beets And Cheese

Serves: 4-6 | Cooking Time: 30 Minutes

Ingredients:

- 1 cup water
- 6 medium beets, trimmed
- Salt and ground black pepper to taste
- ¼ cup cheese (by choice), crumbled

Directions:

1. Pour the water into the Instant Pot and insert a steamer basket.
2. Place the beets in the basket. Close and lock the lid.
3. Select MANUAL and cook at HIGH pressure for 20 minutes.
4. Once cooking is complete, let the pressure Release Naturally for 10 minutes. Release any remaining steam manually. Uncover the pot.
5. Transfer the beets to a bowl and let them cool.
6. Season with salt and pepper and add the blue cheese. Serve.

Pumpkin Puree

Serves: 4-6 | Cooking Time: 30 Minutes

Ingredients:

- 2 lbs small-sized sugar pumpkin, halved and seeds scooped out
- 1 + ¼ cup water
- Salt to taste, optional

Directions:

1. Prepare the Instant Pot by adding 1 cup of water to the pot and placing the steam rack in it.
2. Place the pumpkin halves on the rack. Close and lock the lid.
3. Select MANUAL and cook at HIGH pressure for 14 minutes.
4. When the timer goes off, use a Quick Release. Carefully open the lid.
5. Transfer the pumpkin to a plate and let it cool. Then scoop out the flesh into a bowl.
6. Add ¼ cup of water. Using an immersion blender or food processor, blend until puree.
7. Season with salt and serve.

Steamed Savory Artichokes

Serves: 4 | Cooking Time: 2 Minutes

Ingredients:

- 2 artichokes, trimmed and halved
- 1 lemon, sliced in half
- 2 tablespoons mayonnaise
- 1 teaspoon Dijon mustard
- A pinch of paprika

Directions:

1. Place a steamer basket in the Instant Pot and pour a cup of water
2. Place the artichokes on top of the steamer basket. Spritz the artichokes with lemon juice.
3. Close the lid and press the Steam button.4. Adjust the cooking time to 10 minutes.
4. Do natural pressure release.
5. Meanwhile, mix together mayonnaise, mustard, and paprika.
6. Serve artichokes with the sauce

Curried Carrot And Ginger Soup

Servings:4 | Cooking Time: 40 Minutes

Ingredients:

- 2 teaspoons vegetable oil
- 2 teaspoons peeled and minced fresh ginger
- 5 large carrots, cut into 1-inch pieces
- 1 teaspoon curry powder
- 2 tablespoons dried red lentils, rinsed
- 2 teaspoons kosher salt
- 2½ cups water

Directions:

1. Select Sauté, set the heat to Medium, and add the oil. When it shimmers, add the ginger and carrots and cook, stirring, for about 4 minutes, until the carrots start to brown a bit. Stir in the curry powder, lentils, salt, and water.
2. Lock the lid into place. Select Pressure Cook or Manual; set the pressure to High and the time to 15 minutes.
3. After the cook time is complete, let the pressure release Naturally. Unlock and remove the lid. Using an immersion blender, puree the soup. Mix thoroughly and serve hot.

Kale And Sweet Potatoes With Tofu

Serves: 4 | Cooking Time: 6 Minutes

Ingredients:

- 1 tbsp. tamari sauce
- ⅔ cup vegetable broth
- 1 sweet potato, cubed
- 2 cups chopped kale
- 8 oz. cubed tofu
- Salt and pepper, to taste

Directions:

1. Add tofu in the Instant Pot.
2. Drizzle with half of the tamari and the broth.
3. Cook for about 3 minutes on Sauté function.
4. Add the rest of the ingredients.
5. Lock the lid. Set the Instant Pot to Manual mode, then set the timer for about 3 minutes at High Pressure.
6. Once cooking is complete, do a quick pressure release. Carefully open the lid.
7. Serve immediately!

Steamed Sweet Potatoes With Cilantro

Serves: 4 | Cooking Time: 20 Minutes

Ingredients:

- 2 tbsp butter, melted
- 1 lb sweet potatoes, scrubbed
- 2 tbsp fresh cilantro, chopped

Directions:

1. Pour 1 cup of water in your Instant Pot and fit in a trivet. Place the potatoes on the trivet. Seal the lid, select Manual, and cook for 12 minutes on High pressure. When done, perform a quick pressure release and unlock the lid. Drizzle with melted butter and sprinkle with cilantro to serve.

Emmental Hot Dog Frittata

Serves: 4 | Cooking Time: 25 Minutes

Ingredients:

- 2 turkey hot dogs, sliced
- 1 tbsp butter
- 8 beaten eggs
- 2 tbsp sour cream
- ¼ cup Emmental cheese, grated
- Salt and black pepper to taste

Directions:

1. Grease a baking dish with the butter. Pour 1 cup of water in your Instant Pot and fit in a trivet. Beat eggs and sour cream in a bowl. Mix in Emmental cheese, hot dogs, salt, and pepper. Pour in the dish and cover with aluminum foil. Place on top of the trivet and seal the lid. Select Manual and cook for 15 minutes on High. Once ready, perform a quick pressure release and unlock the lid. Serve warm.

Instant Pot Easy Mushroom Chili

Serves: 3 | Cooking Time: 10 Minutes

Ingredients:

- 2 cups diced tomatoes
- 1 15-ounce can baby Bella mushrooms, chopped
- 2 stalks celery
- 1 tablespoon cumin
- 1 teaspoon Mexican spicy seasoning

Directions:

1. Place all ingredients in the Instant Pot.
2. Stir the contents and close the lid.
3. Close the lid and press the Manual button.
4. Adjust the cooking time to 10 minutes.
5. Do quick pressure release.

Savory Ranch Potatoes

Serves: 2-4 | Cooking Time: 25 Minutes

Ingredients:

- 2 tbsp butter
- 3 large yellow potatoes, cubed
- 2 tbsp Ranch dressing or seasoning mix
- ½ cup water
- Salt and ground black pepper to taste

Directions:

1. Preheat the Instant Pot by selecting Sauté. Once hot, add the butter and melt it.
2. Add the potatoes and stir well.
3. Sprinkle with Ranch seasoning and stir. Add the water. Close and lock the lid.
4. Press the CANCEL button to reset the cooking program, then press the MANUAL button and set the cooking time for 6 minutes at HIGH pressure.
5. When the timer beeps, use a Quick Release. Carefully unlock the lid.

6. Season with salt and pepper and serve.

Cauliflower Mash Dish

Serves: 2-4 | Cooking Time: 20 Minutes

Ingredients:

- 1½ cups water
- 1 cauliflower, florets separated
- Salt and ground black pepper to taste
- 1 tbsp butter
- ½ tsp turmeric
- 2 chives, finely chopped

Directions:

1. Prepare the Instant Pot by adding the water to the pot and placing the steamer basket in it.
2. Put the cauliflower in the basket. Close and lock the lid.
3. Select MANUAL and cook at HIGH pressure for 6 minutes.
4. Once cooking is complete, let the pressure Release Naturally for 2 minutes. Release any remaining steam manually. Uncover the pot.
5. Using a potato masher or fork, mash the cauliflower.
6. Season with salt and pepper. Add in the butter and turmeric and mix well.
7. Top with chopped chives and serve.

Mom's Carrots With Walnuts & Berries

Serves:4 | Cooking Time: 15 Minutes

Ingredients:

- 2 lb carrots, cut into rounds
- ½ cup walnuts, chopped
- 1 tbsp butter
- ¼ cup dried cranberries
- Salt and black pepper to taste
- 1 tbsp vinegar

Directions:

1. Select Sauté and melt the butter. Add in carrots and cook for 5 minutes until tender. Add cranberries, 1 cup of water, and salt. Seal the lid, press Manual, and cook for 3 minutes at High. When done, do a quick pressure release. Pour in the vinegar, and black pepper, and give it a good stir. Scatter the walnuts over and serve.

Butternut Squash Soup

Servings:6 | Cooking Time: 35 Minutes

Ingredients:

- 1 tablespoon extra-virgin olive oil
- 1 cup chopped onion
- ½ teaspoon kosher salt, divided, plus more as needed
- 1 butternut squash, peeled, seeded, and cut into 1-inch chunks
- 6 cups low-sodium vegetable stock, homemade or store-bought
- ½ teaspoon ground ginger
- ¼ teaspoon cayenne pepper

Directions:

1. Select Sauté, set the heat to Medium, and add the olive oil. When it shimmers, add the onion and sprinkle with a pinch or two of salt. Cook, stirring, for about 3 minutes, until the onion begins to soften. Add the butternut squash, stock, remaining salt, ginger, and cayenne and stir to incorporate the spices.
2. Lock the lid into place. Select Pressure Cook or Manual; set the pressure to High and the time to 13 minutes.
3. After the cook time is complete, Quick release the pressure. Unlock and remove the lid. Using an immersion or regular blender, puree the soup.
4. Taste and adjust the seasoning, if needed. Ladle into bowls and serve.

Mushroom & Eggplant Mix

Serves:2 | Cooking Time: 24 Minutes

Ingredients:

- 1 eggplant, sliced
- 2 tbsp olive oil
- 2 garlic cloves, minced
- ½ cup tomatoes, diced
- 1 cup Portobello mushrooms, sliced

Directions:

1. Add olive oil, garlic, and eggplant into the IP and cook on Sauté for 5 minutes. Add in ½ of water and tomatoes. Seal the lid, select Manual at High, and cook for 6 minutes. When done, release the pressure naturally for 5 minutes. Serve hot.

Homemade Coconut Milk Yogurt With Lime & Honey

Serves: 6 | Cooking Time: 15 Hours

Ingredients:

- 2 cans coconut milk
- 1 tbsp gelatin
- 1 tbsp honey
- 1 tbsp probiotic powder
- Zest from 1 lime

Directions:

1. Into the pot, stir in gelatin and coconut milk until well dissolved. Seal the lid, Press Yogurt button until the display is reading "Boil". Once done, the screen will then display "Yogurt". Ensure milk temperature is at 180°F. Remove steel pot from Pressure cooker base and place into a large ice bath to cool milk for 5 minutes to reach 112°F.

2. Remove pot from ice bath and wipe the outside dry. Into the coconut milk mixture, add probiotic powder, honey, and Lime zest, and stir to combine. Return steel pot to the base of the instant pot. Seal the lid, press Yogurt and cook for 10 hours. Once complete, spoon yogurt into clean glass canning jars with rings and lids; place in the refrigerator to chill for 4 hrs to thicken.

One-pot Swiss Chard & Potatoes

Serves: 4 | Cooking Time: 15 Minutes

Ingredients:

- 1 lb Swiss chard, torn, chopped, with stems
- 2 potatoes, peeled, chopped
- ¼ tsp oregano
- 1 tsp salt
- 1 tsp Italian seasoning

Directions:

1. Add Swiss chard and potatoes to the pot. Pour water to cover all and sprinkle with salt. Seal the lid and select Manual/Pressure Cook. Cook for 3 minutes on High. Release the steam naturally, for 5 minutes. Transfer to a serving plate. Sprinkle with oregano and Italian seasoning, to serve.

Instant Pot Mushrooms

Serves: 1 | Cooking Time: 10 Minutes

Ingredients:

- ½ cup water
- 4 oz. mushrooms, sliced
- 2 garlic cloves, minced
- 1 tbsp. olive oil
- Salt and pepper, to taste

Directions:

1. Pour water along with mushrooms in an Instant Pot.
2. Lock the lid. Set the Instant Pot to Manual mode, then set the timer for 5 minutes at High Pressure.
3. Once cooking is complete, do a quick pressure release. Carefully open the lid.
4. Drain the mushroom and then return back to the Instant Pot.
5. Now add olive oil to the pot and mix.
6. Press the Sauté function of the pot and let it cook for 3 minutes.
7. Sauté every 30 seconds.
8. Add the garlic and sauté for 2 minutes or until fragrant. Sprinkle with salt and pepper, then serve the dish.

Spicy Mozzarella Omelet Cups

Serves: 2 | Cooking Time 20 Minutes

Ingredients:

- ¼ cup shredded mozzarella cheese
- 1 tsp olive oil
- 4 eggs, beaten
- Salt and black pepper to taste
- 1 onion, chopped
- 1 spicy chili pepper, chopped

Directions:

1. Grease two ramekins with olive oil. Beat eggs, water, salt, and black pepper in a bowl. Mix in onion and chili pepper. Divide the mixture into the ramekins and top with mozzarella cheese. Pour 1 cup of water in your Instant Pot and fit in a trivet. Place the ramekins on top of the trivet and seal the lid. Select Manual and cook for 15 minutes on High pressure. When ready, perform a quick pressure release and unlock the lid. Serve immediately.

Spicy Cauliflower Cakes

Serves: 4 | Cooking Time: 20 Minutes

Ingredients:
- 1 cauliflower head, chopped
- 1 cup panko breadcrumbs
- 1 cup Parmesan cheese, shredded
- Salt and black pepper to taste
- ½ tsp cayenne pepper
- 2 tbsp olive oil

Directions:

1. Pour 1 cup of water in your Instant Pot and fit in a steamer basket. Place in the cauliflower and seal the lid. Select Manual and cook for 3 minutes on High pressure.

2. Once ready, perform a quick pressure release and unlock the lid. Mash the cauliflower with a fork in a bowl. Add in breadcrumbs, Parmesan cheese, cayenne pepper, salt, and black pepper and mix to combine. Form the meat mixture into patties. Clean the pot and warm the olive oil on Sauté. Fry the cakes for 4-5 minutes, flipping once until golden brown. Serve warm.

Instant Pot Cauliflower Soup

Serves: 4 | Cooking Time: 4 Minutes

Ingredients:
- 1 tablespoon butter
- ½ cup chopped onions
- 1 medium cauliflower, chopped
- 3 cups chicken broth
- Salt and pepper to taste

Directions:

1. Press the Sauté button on the Instant Pot.
2. Heat the butter and sauté the onions.
3. Add the rest of the ingredients.
4. Close the lid and press the Manual button.
5. Adjust the cooking time to 4 minutes.
6. Do quick pressure release.
7. Once the lid is open, place in a blender and puree until smooth.

Instant Pot Steamed Asparagus

Serves: 1 | Cooking Time: 5 Minutes

Ingredients:
- 7 asparagus spears, washed and trimmed
- ¼ tsp. pepper
- 1 tbsp. extra virgin olive oil
- Juice from freshly squeezed ¼ lemon
- ¼ tsp. salt
- 1 cup water

Directions:

1. Place a trivet or the steamer rack in the Instant Pot and pour in the water.
2. In a mixing bowl, combine the asparagus spears, salt, pepper, and lemon juice.
3. Place on top of the trivet.
4. Lock the lid. Set the Instant Pot to Steam mode, then set the timer for 5 minutes at High Pressure.
5. Once cooking is complete, do a quick pressure release. Carefully open the lid.
6. Drizzle the asparagus with olive oil.

Healthy Turnip Alfredo Sauce

Serves: 4 | Cooking Time: 15 Minutes

Ingredients:
- 1 cup water
- 3 medium turnips, peeled and cubed
- 1 cup vegan alfredo sauce
- ½ tsp garlic salt
- 1/3 cup chives, chopped

Directions:

1. Add the water and turnip to the Instant Pot.
2. Close and lock the lid. Select MANUAL and cook at HIGH pressure for 5 minutes.
3. Once timer goes off, use a Quick Release. Carefully unlock the lid.
4. Use a potato masher to mash the turnips.
5. Add the alfredo sauce, garlic salt and chives. Mix well.
6. Serve with veggies or pasta.

Sesame Bok Choy

Serves: 4 | Cooking Time: 4 Minutes

Ingredients:

- 1 tsp. soy sauce
- ½ tsp. sesame oil
- 1½ cups water
- 1 medium Bok choy
- 2 tsps. sesame seeds

Directions:

1. Pour the water into the Instant Pot.
2. Place the Bok choy inside the steamer basket.
3. Lower the basket
4. Lock the lid. Set the Instant Pot to Manual mode, then set the timer for 4 minutes at High Pressure.
5. Once cooking is complete, do a quick pressure release. Carefully open the lid.
6. In a serving bowl, set in the Bok choy. Toss with the remaining ingredients to coat.
7. Serve immediately!

Instant Pot Vegan Stroganoff

Serves: 2 | Cooking Time:10 Minutes

Ingredients:

- 1 ½ cups baby Bella mushrooms, quartered
- 3 cloves of garlic
- 1 cup vegetable stock
- 1 tablespoon sour cream
- Salt and pepper to taste

Directions:

1. Place all ingredients in the Instant Pot.
2. Stir the contents and close the lid.
3. Close the lid and press the Manual button.
4. Adjust the cooking time to 10 minutes.
5. Do quick pressure release.
6. Serve over noodles or rice.

Cottage Cheese Deviled Eggs

Serves:6 | Cooking Time: 15 Minutes

Ingredients:

- 9 large eggs
- ¼ cup Cottage cheese
- ¼ cup mayonnaise
- ¼ tsp garlic powder
- 1 tsp shallot powder
- Salt and black pepper to taste

Directions:

1. Pour 1 cup of water and add a trivet to the pressure cooker. Lay eggs in the steamer basket, and lower the basket onto the trivet. Seal the lid, cook on Manual for 5 minutes at High. Once ready, do a quick pressure release. Transfer the eggs to cold water to cool. Peel, and slice the eggs in half; remove the yolks to a bowl. Mash them with a fork and add the remaining ingredients. Split the mixture on the egg whites and arrange on a Serves: plate.

Rosemary Potato Fries

Serves: 4 | Cooking Time: 25 Minutes

Ingredients:

- 1 lb potatoes, cut into ½ inch sticks
- Sea salt to taste
- 4 tbsp olive oil
- 2 tbsp rosemary, chopped

Directions:

1. Place 1 cup of water in your Instant Pot and fit in a steamer basket. Place the potatoes in the basket and seal the lid. Select Manual and cook for 3 minutes on High pressure.
2. Once ready, perform a quick pressure release and unlock the lid. Remove potatoes to a bowl and pat them dry. Discard the water and dry the pot. Warm the olive oil in the pot on Sauté. Place the potato sticks and cook until golden brown. Sprinkle with sea salt and rosemary and serve right away.

Penne Arrabbiata

Servings:4 | Cooking Time: 30 Minutes

Ingredients:

- 1 tablespoon extra-virgin olive oil
- 1 red onion, diced
- 2 garlic cloves, minced
- 1 can crushed tomatoes
- 1½ cups water
- 10 ounces penne pasta
- ½ to 1 teaspoon red pepper flakes, plus more as needed
- ½ teaspoon kosher salt, plus more as needed
- Freshly ground black pepper

Directions:

1. Select Sauté, set the heat to Medium, and add the olive oil. When it shimmers, add the onion and garlic.

Cook, stirring occasionally, for 4 to 5 minutes, until the onion is softened.

2. Add the tomatoes, water, pasta, red pepper flakes, and salt.

3. Lock the lid into place. Select Pressure Cook or Manual; set the pressure to High and the time to 4 minutes.

4. After the cook time is complete, let the pressure release Naturally for 5 minutes, then Quick release any remaining pressure. Unlock and remove the lid.

5. Taste and season with more salt or red pepper flakes, if needed, and black pepper, then serve.

Breakfast Cheese And Egg Frittatas

Servings:x | Cooking Time: 10 Minutes

Ingredients:

- 4 eggs
- 4 tablespoons milk
- 1/2 teaspoon cayenne pepper
- Sea salt and ground black pepper, to taste
- 1/4 cup cream cheese

Directions:

1. Place 1 cup of water and a metal trivet in the inner pot.

2. Mix all ingredients until everything is well incorporated. Pour the egg mixture into silicone molds.

3. Lower the molds onto the prepared trivet.

4. Secure the lid. Choose the "Manual" mode and cook for 5 minutes at High pressure. Once cooking is complete, use a quick pressure release; carefully remove the lid. Bon appétit!

Crushed Potatoes With Aioli

Serves: 4 | Cooking Time: 25 Minutes

Ingredients:

- 1 lb Russet potatoes, pierced
- Salt and black pepper to taste
- 2 tbsp olive oil
- 4 tbsp mayonnaise
- 1 tsp garlic paste
- 1 tbsp lemon juice

Directions:

1. Mix olive oil, salt, and pepper in a bowl. Add in the potatoes and toss to coat. Pour 1 cup of water in your Instant Pot and fit in a trivet. Place the potatoes on the

trivet and seal the lid. Select Manual and cook for 12 minutes on High.

2. Once ready, perform a quick pressure release and unlock the lid. In a small bowl, combine mayonnaise, garlic paste, and lemon juice; mix well. Peel and crush the potatoes and transfer to a serving bowl. Serve with aioli.

Veggie Flax Patties

Serves:4 | Cooking Time: 30 Minutes

Ingredients:

- 2 tbsp canola oil
- 1 bag frozen mixed veggies
- 1 cup cauliflower florets
- Salt and black pepper to taste
- 1 tbsp cumin
- 1 cup flax meal

Directions:

1. Pour 1 cup of water in your IP. Combine mixed veggies and cauliflower florets in a steamer basket and then lower the basket inside the pot. Seal the lid, select Manual and cook for 5 minutes at High. After the timer goes off, do a quick pressure release. Transfer the veggies to a bowl and discard the water. Mash the veggies with a potato masher, add cumin and allow them to cool for 10 minutes. When safe to handle, stir in the flax meal and shape the mixture into 4 equal patties. Wipe the pot clean and add canola oil. Set to Sauté. Add veggie burgers, and cook for 6 minutes, flipping once halfway through cooking. Serve.

Paleo Crusted Veggie Quiche

Serves:4 | Cooking Time: 25 Minutes

Ingredients:

- 4 oz goat cheese, crumbled
- 8 eggs
- 2 cups mushrooms, sliced
- 1 ½ cups kale, chopped
- 1 tbsp butter, melted
- Salt and black pepper to taste

Directions:

1. In a bowl, whisk eggs, black pepper, and salt until well smooth. Grease a baking dish with melted butter and add the mushrooms and kale. Pour the egg mixture over and top with the cheese. Add 1 cup of water and a trivet to the pot and lay the dish on the trivet. Seal the

lid, select Manual at High, and cook for 15 minutes. When done, release the pressure naturally for 5 minutes. Serve hot.

Tofu Hash Brown Breakfast

Serves: 4 | Cooking Time: 15 Minutes

Ingredients:

- 1 cup tofu cubes
- 2 cups frozen hash browns
- 8 beaten eggs
- 1 cup shredded cheddar cheese
- ¼ cup milk
- Salt and black pepper to taste

Directions:

1. Set your Instant Pot to Sauté. Place in tofu and cook until browned. Add in hash brown and cook for 2 minutes. Beat eggs, cheddar cheese, milk, salt, and pepper in a bowl and pour over hash brown. Seal the lid, select Manual, and cook for 5 minutes on High. Once done, perform a quick pressure release. Cut into slices before serving.

Puréed Chili Carrots

Serves: 4 | Cooking Time:5 Minutes

Ingredients:

- 1½ cups water
- 1 tbsp. maple syrup
- 1 tbsp. coconut oil
- 1½ lbs. carrots, chopped
- 1 tsp. chili powder

Directions:

1. Pour the water into the Instant Pot.
2. Place the chopped carrots inside the steamer basket.
3. Arrange the basket in the Instant Pot.
4. Lock the lid. Set the Instant Pot to Manual mode, then set the timer for 4 minutes on High Pressure.
5. Once cooking is complete, do a quick pressure release. Carefully open the lid.
6. Transfer the carrots along with the remaining ingredients to a food processor.
7. Process until puréed and smooth.
8. Serve immediately!

Brussels Sprouts And Pomegranate

Serves: 2-4 | Cooking Time: 20 Minutes

Ingredients:

- 1 cup water
- 1 lb Brussels sprouts, trimmed and cut into half
- Salt and ground black pepper to taste
- ¼ cup pine nuts, toasted
- 1 pomegranate, seeds separated
- 1 tsp olive oil

Directions:

1. Pour the water into the Instant Pot and insert a steamer basket.
2. Place the Brussels sprouts in the basket.
3. Close and lock the lid. Select MANUAL and cook at HIGH pressure for 4 minutes.
4. When the timer beeps, use a Quick Release. Carefully unlock the lid.
5. Transfer the sprouts to a serving plate.
6. Season with salt, pepper and pine nuts. Add the pomegranate seeds and stir.
7. Drizzle with oil and stir well. Serve.

Cauliflower Patties

Serves: 4 | Cooking Time: 30 Minutes

Ingredients:

- 1½ cups water
- 1 cauliflower head, chopped
- 1 cup ground almonds
- 1 cup vegan cheese, shredded
- Salt and ground black pepper to taste
- 2 tbsp olive oil

Directions:

1. Pour the water into the Instant Pot and insert a steamer basket.
2. Put the cauliflower in to the basket.
3. Close and lock the lid. Select MANUAL and cook at HIGH pressure for 5 minutes.
4. Once timer goes off, use a Quick Release. Carefully unlock the lid.
5. Place the cauliflower in a food processor and ground it.
6. Add the almonds and cheese. Season with salt and pepper. Mix well.
7. Shape the mixture into oval patties each ½ inch

thick.

8. Carefully pour the water out of the pot and completely dry the pot before replacing it.
9. Select the SAUTÉ setting on the Instant Pot and heat the oil.
10. Add the patties and cook on both sides until golden. You may have to do it in two batches.
11. Serve.

Curried Squash Stew

Serves: 10 | Cooking Time: 10 Minutes

Ingredients:

• 2 cups squash, chopped
• 1 can full-fat coconut milk
• 2 tablespoon garam masala
• Salt and pepper to taste
• 1 bag baby spinach, rinsed

Directions:

1. Place all ingredients except for the spinach in the Instant Pot.
2. Stir the contents and close the lid.
3. Close the lid and press the Manual button.
4. Adjust the cooking time to 10 minutes.
5. Do quick pressure release.
6. Once the lid is open, press the Sauté button.
7. Add the spinach and continue cooking until the greens have wilted.

Steamed Lemon Artichokes

Serves: 4 | Cooking Time: 20 Minutes

Ingredients:

• 1 cup water
• 2 garlic cloves, minced
• Salt, to taste
• 1 bay leaf
• 4 artichokes, trimmed
• 2 tbsps. freshly squeezed lemon juice

Directions:

1. Mix the water, garlic, salt and bay leaf inside the Instant Pot.
2. Place steamer basket in the pot.
3. Add the artichokes.
4. Drizzle each one with lemon juice.
5. Lock the lid. Set the Instant Pot to Steam mode, then set the timer for 10 minutes at High Pressure.
6. Once cooking is complete, do a quick pressure re-
lease. Carefully open the lid.
7. Remove outer petals and discard.
8. Discard the bay leaf, slice the artichokes into pieces and serve.

Coconut Cauliflower Rice

Serves: 3 | Cooking Time: 10 Minutes

Ingredients:

• 1 onion, chopped
• Salt and pepper, to taste
• 3 garlic cloves, minced
• 1 cauliflower head, grated
• 1 cup freshly squeezed coconut milk

Directions:

1. Put the cauliflower florets in a food processor and pulse to rice the cauliflower.
2. Place the riced cauliflower and remaining ingredients in the Instant Pot.
3. Lock the lid. Set the Instant Pot to Manual mode, then set the timer for 10 minutes at High Pressure.
4. Once cooking is complete, do a quick pressure release. Carefully open the lid.
5. Serve warm.

Smoked Kielbasa Baked Eggs

Servings: 2 | Cooking Time: 10 Minutes

Ingredients:

• ½ cup diced smoked kielbasa sausages
• ½ cup hash brown potatoes
• ¼ cup shredded cheddar
• 4 eggs, cracked into a bowl
• 1 tbsp chopped scallions
• Salt and black pepper to taste

Directions:

1. Grease a large ramekin with cooking spray and lay in ingredients in this order: sausages, hash browns, and cheddar cheese. Create a hole in the center and pour in eggs. Scatter scallions on top and season with salt and pepper. Pour 1 cup water into the inner pot and fit in a trivet. Place ramekin on the trivet, seal the lid, select Manual/Pressure Cook on High, and set the time to 2 minutes. When done, do a quick release. Carefully remove ramekin and serve.

Pasta & Rice Recipes

Pasta & Rice Recipes

Madagascar Pink Rice

Serves: 4-6 | Cooking Time: 25 Minutes

Ingredients:

- 1 cups pink rice
- 1 cups water
- ½ tsp salt

Directions:

1. Rinse the rice well.
2. Add the rice, water and salt to the Instant Pot, stir.
3. Close and secure the lid. Select the MANUAL setting and set the cooking time for 5 minutes at HIGH pressure.
4. When the timer goes off, let the pressure Release Naturally for 10 minutes, then release any remaining steam manually. Open the pot.
5. Fluff the rice with the rice spatula or fork. Serve.

Family Truffle Popcorn

Serves: 4 | Cooking Time: 15 Minutes

Ingredients:

- 1 stick butter
- 1 cup popcorn kernels
- 1 tablespoon truffle oil
- 1/4 cup parmesan cheese, grated
- Sea salt, to taste

Directions:

1. Press the "Sauté" button and melt the butter. Stir until it begins to simmer.
2. Stir in the popcorn kernels and cover. When the popping slows down, press the "Cancel" button.
3. Now, add the truffle oil, parmesan, and sea salt. Toss to combine and serve immediately.

Movie Night Popcorn

Serves: 4 | Cooking Time:15 Minutes

Ingredients:

- 1/4 cup parmesan cheese, grated
- 1 cup popcorn kernels
- 1 tablespoon truffle oil
- 1 stick butter
- Sea salt, to taste

Directions:

1. Press the "Sauté" button and melt the butter. Stir until it begins to simmer.
2. Stir in the popcorn kernels and cover. When the popping slows down, press the "Cancel" button.
3. Now, add the truffle oil, parmesan, and sea salt. Toss to combine and serve immediately.

Parsley Jasmine Rice

Serves: 2-4 | Cooking Time: 25 Minutes

Ingredients:

- 2 cups jasmine rice
- 3 ½ cups water
- Salt and black pepper to taste
- Parsley to garnish

Directions:

1. Stir rice and water in the cooker. Season with Salt to taste. Seal the lid and cook for 15 minutes on High Pressure.Release Pressure naturally for 10 minutes. Use a fork to fluff rice. Add black pepper and parsley before serving.

Sweet Pearl Onion Mix

Serves: 4 | Cooking Time: 5 Minutes

Ingredients:

- 4 tbsps. balsamic vinegar
- 1 tbsp. sugar
- 1 lb. pearl onions
- ½ cup water
- ¼ tsp. salt

Directions:

1. In the Instant Pot, mix pearl onions with salt, water, vinegar and sugar, stir.
2. Lock the lid. Select the Manual mode, then set the timer for 5 minutes on Low Pressure.
3. Once the timer goes off, perform a quick release. Carefully open the lid.
4. Toss onions again, divide them between plates and serve as a side dish.

Chestnut Mushrooms

Serves: 4 | Cooking Time: 10 Minutes

Ingredients:

- 2 lbs. halved mushrooms
- ½ cup vegetable soup
- 1 tsp. Worcestershire sauce
- 1 cup halved jarred chestnuts
- 6 bacon slices, chopped

Directions:

1. Set the Instant Pot to Sauté, add bacon, stir and cook for 5 minutes on both sides.
2. Stir in the chestnuts and sauté for 1 more minute.
3. Add mushrooms, Worcestershire sauce and soup, stir.
4. Lock the lid. Select the Manual mode, then set the timer for 8 minutes at High Pressure.
5. Once the timer goes off, perform a quick release. Carefully open the lid.
6. Enjoy as a side dish.

Easy Jasmine Rice

Serves: 4-6 | Cooking Time: 25 Minutes

Ingredients:

- 2 cups jasmine rice
- 2 cups water
- 2 tsp olive oil
- ½ tsp salt

Directions:

1. Rinse the rice well.
2. Transfer the rice to the Instant Pot. Add the water, oil and salt and stir.
3. Close and secure the lid. Select MANUAL and cook at HIGH pressure for 4 minutes.
4. Once timer goes off, allow to Naturally Release for 10 minutes, then release the remaining pressure manually. Open the lid.
5. Fluff the rice with a fork and serve.

Creamy Spinach

Serves: 4 | Cooking Time: 6 Minutes

Ingredients:

- Ground nutmeg
- 10 oz. spinach, roughly chopped
- 2 shallots, chopped
- 2 cups heavy cream
- 2 tbsps. butter

Directions:

1. Set the Instant Pot to Sauté, add butter, melt it, add shallots, stir and cook for 2 minutes.
2. Add spinach, stir, and cook for 30 seconds more.
3. Add cream and nutmeg, stir.
4. Lock the lid. Select the Manual mode, then set the timer for 3 minutes at High Pressure.
5. Once the timer goes off, perform a quick release. Carefully open the lid.
6. Divide everything between plates and serve as a side dish.

Brown Rice Salad

Serves: 2 | Cooking Time: 20 Minutes

Ingredients:

- ½ cup mung beans
- 1 tsp. lemon juice
- ½ tsp. cumin seeds
- ½ cup brown rice
- 4 cups water

Directions:

1. In the Instant Pot, mix mung beans with rice, water, lemon juice and cumin, stir.
2. Lock the lid. Select the Manual mode, then set the timer for 20 minutes at Low Pressure.
3. Once the timer goes off, perform a quick release. Carefully open the lid.
4. Enjoy the side dish!

Arborio Rice Side Salad

Serves: 4 | Cooking Time: 4 Minutes

Ingredients:

- 1 bunch basil, chopped
- 4 cups water
- 2 cups Arborio rice
- ¼ tsp. salt
- 1 cup pitted and sliced black olives in oil

Directions:

1. In the Instant Pot, mix rice with water.
2. Lock the lid. Select the Manual mode, then set the timer for 20 minutes at Low Pressure.
3. Once the timer goes off, perform a natural release for 10 minutes, then release any remaining pressure. Carefully open the lid.
4. Drain and transfer to a salad bowl.
5. Add a pinch of salt, olives and basil, toss well, divide between plates and serve as a side salad.

Brussels Sprouts And Chestnuts

Serves: 5 | Cooking Time: 5 Minutes

Ingredients:

- 3 tbsps. olive oil
- ¼ cup vegetable soup
- 1 red vinegar splash
- 2 lbs. halved Brussels sprouts
- 1 cup halved jarred chestnuts

Directions:

1. Set the Instant Pot to Sauté. Heat the oil and add Brussels sprouts, stir and cook for 2 minutes.
2. Add chestnuts, stock and vinegar, stir.
3. Lock the lid. Select the Manual mode, then set the timer for 3 minutes at High Pressure.
4. Once the timer goes off, perform a quick release. Carefully open the lid.
5. Enjoy the side dish.

Breakfast Millet Porridge

Serves: 5 | Cooking Time:25 Minutes

Ingredients:

- 1/4 cup almonds, roughly chopped
- 1/2 cup golden raisins
- 1 tablespoon orange juice
- A pinch of sea salt
- 3 cups water
- 1 ½ cups millet

Directions:

1. Place all ingredients in the inner pot of your Instant Pot and close the lid.
2. Secure the lid. Choose the "Manual" mode and cook for 12 minutes at High pressure. Once cooking is complete, use a natural pressure release for 10 minutes; carefully remove the lid.
3. Taste and adjust the seasonings. Bon appétit!

Kale Sauté

Serves: 4 | Cooking Time: 7 Minutes

Ingredients:

- 1 tbsp. olive oil
- 3 garlic cloves
- ½ cup veggie stock
- Juice of ½ lemon
- 1 lb. kale, trimmed

Directions:

1. Set the Instant Pot to Sauté. Heat the oil and add garlic, stir and cook for 2 minutes.
2. Add kale, stock and lemon juice, stir a bit.
3. Lock the lid. Select the Manual mode, then set the timer for 5 minutes at High Pressure.
4. Once the timer goes off, perform a quick release. Carefully open the lid.
5. Stir and divide between plates and serve as a side dish.

Tasty Vidalia Onions Mix

Serves: 4 | Cooking Time: 15 Minutes

Ingredients:

- 2 tbsps. butter
- 4 Vidalia onions, sliced
- 1 tbsp. chopped sage
- ¼ cup chicken stock
- ½ cup cornbread stuffing cubes

Directions:

1. Set the Instant Pot to Sauté, add butter, melt it, add onions and sage, toss a bit and cook for 3 minutes.
2. Add stock, stir.
3. Lock the lid. Select the Manual mode, then set the timer for 7 minutes at High Pressure.
4. Once the timer goes off, perform a quick release. Carefully open the lid.
5. Add cornbread stuffing cubes, set the pot in Sauté mode again, toss and cook everything for 3 to 4 minutes more.
6. Serve as a side dish!

Tasty Mushrooms And Rosemary

Serves: 6 | Cooking Time: 10 Minutes

Ingredients:

- ½ cup white wine
- 3 lbs. mixed mushroom caps
- 3 rosemary sprigs, chopped
- 4 garlic cloves, minced
- ¾ cup olive oil

Directions:

1. Set the Instant Pot to Sauté, add oil, heat, add garlic and rosemary, stir and cook for 2 to 3 minutes.
2. Add mushroom caps and wine, stir.
3. Lock the lid. Select the Manual mode, then set the timer for 7 to 8 minutes at High Pressure.
4. Once the timer goes off, perform a quick release. Carefully open the lid.
5. Stir mushroom mix again, divide between plates and serve as a side dish.

Brown Rice

Serves: 4-6 | Cooking Time: 30 Minutes

Ingredients:

- 2 cups brown rice
- 2 cups vegetable broth or water
- ½ tsp salt

Directions:

1. Add the rice, broth and salt to the Instant Pot and stir.
2. Close and secure the lid. Select MANUAL and cook at HIGH pressure for 21 minutes.
3. When the timer goes off, let the pressure Release Naturally for 10 minutes, then release any remaining steam manually.
4. Carefully open the lid. Fluff the rice with the rice spatula or fork. Serve.

Traditional Jowar Ki Kheer

Serves: 3 | Cooking Time: 25 Minutes

Ingredients:

- 1 cup dried sorghum
- 3 cups soy milk
- 1 tablespoon ghee
- 1/2 cup brown sugar
- 1/2 cup cashews, roughly chopped

Directions:

1. Place the dries sorghum, milk, ghee, and brown sugar in the inner pot.
2. Secure the lid. Choose the "Porridge" mode and cook for 20 minutes at High pressure. Once cooking is complete, use a quick pressure release; carefully remove the lid.
3. Serve in individual bowls garnished with chopped cashews. Enjoy!

Broccoli Couscous

Serves: 4 | Cooking Time: 15 Minutes

Ingredients:

- 1 head broccoli, cut into florets
- 2 tbsp butter, melted
- 1 cup couscous
- Salt and black pepper to taste
- Parsley leaves, chopped

Directions:

1. Pour 1 cup of water in the Instant Pot and add a steamer basket. Place the broccoli in the basket and close and secure the lid. Select Steam and cook for 3 minutes on High. Once pressure cooking is complete, use a quick release.
2. In a bowl cover couscous with salted boiled water. Let it stand for 2-3 minutes until the water has absorbed. Fluff with a fork and stir in broccoli, adjust the seasoning with salt and pepper. Top with parsley and serve.

Simple Spinach Side Dish

Serves: 3 | Cooking Time: 5 Minutes

Ingredients:

- ½ tsp. turmeric powder
- 1 tsp. olive oil
- 6 oz. spinach leaves
- ½ cup vegetable soup
- ½ tsp. garam masala

Directions:

1. Set the Instant Pot to Sauté and heat the olive oil. Add spinach, stir and toss for 1 to 2 minutes.
2. Add garam masala, turmeric and soup, stir.
3. Lock the lid. Select the Manual mode, then set the timer for 3 minutes at High Pressure.
4. Once the timer goes off, perform a quick release. Carefully open the lid.

5. Serve as a side dish!

French Butter Rice

Serves: 4-6 | Cooking Time: 45 Minutes

Ingredients:
- 1 stick (½ cup) butter
- 2 cups brown rice
- 1 cups vegetable stock
- 1½ cups French onion soup

Directions:

1. To preheat the Instant Pot, select SAUTÉ. Once hot, add the butter and melt it.
2. Add the rice, vegetable stock, onion soup and stir to combine.
3. Close and secure the lid. Select the MANUAL setting and set the cooking time for 22 minutes at HIGH pressure.
4. Once cooking is complete, let Naturally Release for 10 minutes. Release any remaining steam manually. Open the lid.
5. Serve. If you like, you can garnish the rice with parsley.

Multi-grain Rice Millet Blend

Serves: 4-6 | Cooking Time: 15 Minutes

Ingredients:
- 2 cups jasmine rice or long-grain white rice
- ½ cup millet
- 3¼ cups water
- ½ tsp sea salt (optional)

Directions:

1. Put the rice, millet, water and salt in the Instant Pot and stir.
2. Close and secure the lid. Select the RICE setting and set the cooking time for 10 minutes.
3. When the timer goes off, use a Quick Release.
4. Carefully open the lid. Fluff the dish with the rice spatula or fork. Serve.

Pasta With Broccoli

Serves: 4 | Cooking Time: 20 Minutes

Ingredients:
- ½ lb pasta
- 2 cups water
- ½ cup broccoli
- 8 oz cheddar cheese, grated
- ½ cup half and half
- Salt to taste

Directions:

1. Add pasta and water to the Instant Pot.
2. Place a steamer basket on top.
3. Put the broccoli in the basket. Close and lock the lid.
4. Select MANUAL and cook at HIGH pressure for 4 minutes.
5. When the timer goes off, use a Quick Release. Carefully open the lid.
6. Take out the broccoli and drain the pasta.
7. Set your Instant Pot on SAUTÉ mode. Add the cooked pasta, broccoli, cheese and half and half, stir well. Season with salt to taste. Cook the dish for 2 minutes.
8. Serve.

Chicken Alfredo Pasta

Serves: 2 | Cooking Time: 15 Minutes

Ingredients:
- 8 oz fettuccine, halved
- 2 cups water
- 2 tsp chicken seasoning
- 1 jar (15 oz) Alfredo sauce
- 1 cup cooked and diced chicken
- Salt and ground black pepper to taste

Directions:

1. Pout the water in the Instant Pot and add the pasta and chicken seasoning. Stir well.
2. Close and lock the lid. Select MANUAL and cook at HIGH pressure for 3 minutes.
3. Once pressure cooking is complete, use a Quick Release. Unlock and carefully open the lid.
4. Drain the pasta and add to serving bowl.
5. Add the sauce and cooked chicken. Season with salt and pepper to taste.
6. Stir well and serve.

Simple Corn Side Dish

Serves: 4 | Cooking Time: 12 Minutes

Ingredients:
- 2 tbsps. butter
- 3 garlic cloves, minced
- 2 cups corn kernels
- 6 oz. cream cheese
- ⅓ cup milk

Directions:

1. Set the Instant Pot to Sauté, add butter, melt it, add garlic, stir and cook for 2 minutes.
2. Stir in the corn and let cook for 2 additional minutes.
3. Add cream cheese and milk, stir.
4. Lock the lid. Select the Manual mode, then set the timer for 7 minutes at High Pressure.
5. Once the timer goes off, perform a quick release. Carefully open the lid.
6. Toss creamy corn one more time, divide between plates and serve as a side dish.

Yogurt Chicken Pilaf With Quinoa

Serves: 2-4 | Cooking Time: 60 Minutes

Ingredients:
- 1 lb chicken breasts, boneless, skinless
- 1 cup quinoa
- 2 cups chicken broth
- Salt and black pepper to taste
- Greek yogurt for topping

Directions:

1. Add chicken and broth to the pot and seal the lid. Cook on Poultry for 15 minutes on High. Do a quick release and remove the chicken. Add quinoa and seal the lid. Cook on Rice mode for 8 minutes on High. Cut the chicken meat into bite-sized pieces and place in a large bowl. To the cooker, do a quick release. Stir in chicken, to warm, season with black pepper. and top with greek yogurt.

Tasty Maple Acorn Squash Dish

Serves: 4 | Cooking Time: 10 Minutes

Ingredients:
- 2 tsps. sriracha sauce
- ¼ cup maple syrup
- 4 thyme sprigs, chopped
- 3 tbsps. butter
- 2 halved acorn squash

Directions:

1. Set the Instant Pot to Sauté, add butter, melt it, add acorn squash wedges, stir and cook for 1 to 2 minutes.
2. Add maple syrup, sriracha sauce and thyme, stir.
3. Lock the lid. Select the Manual mode, then set the timer for 8 minutes at High Pressure.
4. Once the timer goes off, perform a quick release. Carefully open the lid.
5. Toss squash wedges gently, divide between plates and serve as a side dish.

Brown Rice With Sunflower Seeds

Serves: 2 | Cooking Time: 30 Minutes

Ingredients:
- ½ cup brown rice
- 1 cup chicken broth
- ⅓ tsp lemon juice
- 1 tsp olive oil
- ½ tbsp toasted sunflower seeds

Directions:

1. Add broth and brown rice, seal the lid, press Manual and cook for 15 minutes. Release the pressure quickly. Do not open the lid for an additional 5 minutes. Use a fork to fluff rice. Add lemon juice, sunflower seeds and oil.

Cauliflower And Pineapple Rice

Serves: 4-6 | Cooking Time: 40 Minutes

Ingredients:

- 2 tsp extra virgin olive oil
- 4 cups water
- 2 cups jasmine rice
- 1 cauliflower, florets separated and chopped
- ½ pineapple, peeled and chopped
- Salt and ground black pepper to taste

Directions:

1. Combine all of the ingredients in the Instant Pot and stir to combine.
2. Close and secure the lid. Select the MANUAL setting and set the cooking time for 20 minutes at LOW pressure.
3. Once pressure cooking is complete, let Naturally Release for 10 minutes, then quick release remaining pressure.
4. Carefully open the pot. Fluff the dish with the rice spatula or fork. Serve.

Radishes Side Salad

Serves: 3 | Cooking Time: 8 Minutes

Ingredients:

- 2 chopped bacon slices
- ½ cup veggie stock
- 2 tbsps. sour cream
- 1 tbsp. chopped green onions
- 7 oz. halved red radishes

Directions:

1. Set the Instant Pot to Sauté, add bacon, stir and cook for 6 minutes on both sides.
2. Add radishes and stock, stir.
3. Lock the lid. Select the Manual mode, then set the timer for 4 minutes at High Pressure.
4. Once the timer goes off, perform a quick release. Carefully open the lid.
5. Add sour cream and green onions, stir.
6. Lock the lid, then set the timer for 2 minutes.
7. Divide between plates and serve as a side dish.

Delicious Shiitake Mushrooms Mix

Serves: 4 | Cooking Time: 10 Minutes

Ingredients:

- 2 tsps. ginger
- 1 cup veggie stock
- 1 lb. shiitake mushroom caps, quartered
- 2 tbsps. butter
- 2 cups edamame

Directions:

1. Set the Instant Pot to Sauté, add butter, melt it, add ginger, stir and cook for 30 seconds.
2. Add mushrooms, stir and cook for 1 to 2 minutes.
3. Add edamame and stock, stir.
4. Lock the lid. Select the Manual mode, then set the timer for 8 minutes at High Pressure.
5. Once the timer goes off, perform a quick release. Carefully open the lid.
6. Serve as a side dish.

Soups, Stews & Chilis Recipes

Soups, Stews & Chilis Recipes

Cauliflower Soup

Serves: 4 | Cooking Time: 25 Minutes

Ingredients:

- 1 tbsp butter
- 1 large onion, chopped
- 3 cups chicken broth
- 1 medium cauliflower, chopped
- Salt and ground black pepper to taste

Directions:

1. Preheat the Instant Pot by selecting SAUTÉ. Once hot, add the butter and melt it.
2. Add the onion and sauté for 4-5 minutes, until softened.
3. Add the broth, cauliflower, salt and pepper. Stir well. Close and lock the lid.
4. Press the CANCEL button to stop the SAUTE function, then select the MANUAL setting and set the cooking time for 5 minutes at HIGH pressure.
5. Once timer goes off, use a Quick Release. Carefully unlock the lid.
6. With an immersion blender, blend the soup to your desired texture. Serve.

Lemon Chicken Soup

Serves: 4 | Cooking Time: 8 Minutes

Ingredients:

- 2 tbsps. lemon juice
- 6 cups chicken stock
- 3 chicken breast fillets
- 1 tsp. garlic powder
- 1 diced onion
- Salt and pepper, to taste

Directions:

1. Put the chicken stock, chicken breast fillets, garlic powder, and onion in the Instant Pot and mix well.
2. Lock the lid. Select the Manual mode, then set the timer for 6 minutes at High Pressure.
3. Once the timer goes off, do a natural pressure release for 5 minutes, then release any remaining pressure. Carefully open the lid.
4. Remove the chicken and shred.
5. Put it back to the pot and set the Instant Pot to Sau-

té.
6. Whisk in the lemon juice. Season with salt and pepper. Serve immediately.

Chicken, Mushroom & Spinach Stew

Serves:4 | Cooking Time: 35 Minutes

Ingredients:

- 2 portobello mushrooms, sliced
- 4 chicken fillets
- Black pepper and salt to taste
- 4 cups baby spinach, chopped
- ½ cup chives, chopped
- 4 tbsp olive oil

Directions:

1. Season chicken on both sides. Heat olive oil on Sauté in the IP. Add chicken and cook for 5 minutes in total. Stir in vegetables and pour in 1 cup of water. Seal the lid, select Manual at High and cook for 20 minutes. When ready, release the pressure naturally for 5 minutes. Serve garnished with chopped chives on top.

Fish Soup

Serves: 4 | Cooking Time: 8 Minutes

Ingredients:

- 1 lb. boneless, skinless and cubed white fish fillets
- 1 carrot, chopped
- 1 cup chopped bacon
- 4 cups chicken stock
- Salt and pepper, to taste
- 2 cups heavy whipping cream

Directions:

1. In the Instant Pot, mix the fish with carrot, bacon and stock. Sprinkle with salt and pepper. Stir to combine well.
2. Lock the lid. Set to Manual function and set the timer for 5 minutes at Low Pressure.
3. Once the timer goes off, press Cancel. Do a quick pressure release.
4. Carefully open the lid. Add the cream, stir, set the pot to Sauté, cook for 3 minutes more, ladle the soup into bowls and serve.

Creamy Broccoli Chicken Bone Soup

Serves: 5 | Cooking Time: 34 Minutes

Ingredients:

- ½ lb. chicken bones
- 4 cups water
- Salt and pepper, to taste
- 2 heads broccoli, cut into florets
- 1 small avocado, sliced
- 1 tsp. paprika powder

Directions:

1. Place the chicken bones and water in the Instant Pot.
2. Sprinkle salt and pepper for seasoning
3. Lock the lid. Set on the Manual mode, then set the timer to 30 minutes at High Pressure.
4. When the timer goes off, do a natural pressure release for 10 minutes, then release any remaining pressure.
5. Carefully open the lid, then discard the bones with tongs.
6. Add the broccoli.
7. Close the lid again and press the Manual button and cook for 4 minutes at Low Pressure.
8. When the timer goes off, do a quick pressure release.
9. Transfer the soup into a blender, then add avocado slices.
10. Pulse until smooth and set in a bowl.
11. Sprinkle with paprika powder.
12. Serve immediately.

Black Bean Soup

Serves: 4 | Cooking Time: 20 Minutes

Ingredients:

- 2½ cups salsa
- 45 oz. canned black beans and juice
- ½ cup chopped cilantro
- 1 garlic clove
- 2 cups water
- 2 tsps. ground cumin

Directions:

1. In the Instant Pot, mix the salsa with black beans, cilantro, garlic, water, and cumin, stir to combine well.
2. Lock the lid. Select the Manual mode, then set the timer for 15 minutes at High Pressure.

3. Once the timer goes off, do a quick pressure release.
4. Carefully open the lid. Stir soup one more time, then ladle into bowls and serve.

Beef Tomato Stew

Serves: 4 | Cooking Time: 30 Minutes

Ingredients:

- 2 tsps. olive oil
- 1 lb. lean beef stew meat
- 2 cups diced tomatoes
- 2 spring onions, chopped
- 4 cups low-sodium beef broth
- Salt and pepper, to taste

Directions:

1. Press the Sauté bottom on the Instant Pot.
2. Add and heat the olive oil.
3. Add the meat and sauté for 3 to 4 minutes to evenly brown.
4. Add the tomatoes and onions, then sauté for 3 to 4 minutes or until soft.
5. Pour in the broth. Sprinkle with salt and pepper.
6. Lock the lid. Press Meat/Stew bottom. Set the timer to 20 minutes at High Pressure.
7. Once the timer goes off, press Cancel. Do a quick pressure release.
8. Open the lid, transfer them in a large bowl and serve.

Veal And Buckwheat Groat Stew

Serves: 4 | Cooking Time: 50 Minutes

Ingredients:

- ¼ cup buckwheat groats
- 1 tsp. olive oil
- 1 onion, chopped
- 7 oz. veal shoulder
- 3 cups low-sodium beef stock
- Salt and pepper, to taste

Directions:

1. Add the buckwheat and pour in enough water to cover the buckwheat in the Instant Pot. Stir the ingredients to combine well.
2. Lock the lid. Press Manual. Set the timer to 12 minutes at Low Pressure.
3. Once the timer goes off, press Cancel. Do a natural pressure release, then release any remaining pressure.
4. Drain water and set the buckwheat aside.

5. Press the Sauté bottom on the Instant Pot.
6. Add and heat the olive oil.
7. Add the onions and cook for 3 minutes until translucent.
8. Add the veal shoulder and sauté for 4 to 5 minutes to evenly brown.
9. Pour in the beef stock. Sprinkle with salt and pepper.
10. Lock the lid. Press Manual. Set the timer to 30 minutes at High Pressure.
11. Once the timer goes off, press Cancel. Do a natural pressure release for 8 to 10 minutes.
12. Open the lid, mix in the buckwheat and transfer them in a large bowl and serve.

Minestrone

Serves: 4 | Cooking Time: 6 Minutes

Ingredients:

- 27 oz. tomato paste
- 15 oz. drained canned cannellini beans
- 2 cups vegetable soup
- 1 cup cooked orzo pasta
- ¼ cup grated Parmesan cheese

Directions:

1. In the Instant Pot, mix the tomato paste with beans and vegetable soup, stir to combine well.
2. Lock the lid. Set to the Manual mode and set the timer for 6 minutes at High Pressure.
3. Once the timer goes off, do a natural pressure release for 10 minutes, then release any remaining pressure.
4. Carefully open the lid. Add the orzo pasta and stir, then ladle the soup into bowls and serve with Parmesan sprinkled on top.

Asparagus Soup

Serves: 4 | Cooking Time: 55 Minutes

Ingredients:

- 1 tbsp. ghee
- 1 medium onion, chopped
- 1 garlic clove, minced
- 1 cup diced ham
- Salt and pepepr, to taste
- 2 lbs. halved asparagus
- Salt and pepper, to taste

Directions:

1. Set the Instant Pot to Sauté and melt the ghee.
2. Add the onions and garlic and cook for about 5 minutes
3. Add the diced ham, salt and pepper, and let it simmer for 2 to 3 minutes.
4. Add the asparagus.
5. Lock the lid. Select the Soup mode, then set the timer 45 minutes at High Pressure.
6. Once the timer goes off, do a quick pressure release. Carefully open the lid.
7. Transfer the soup to a food processor and pulse until smooth.
8. Serve warm.

Pumpkin Soup

Serves: 4 | Cooking Time: 8 Minutes

Ingredients:

- 1 tsp. garlic powder
- 2 cups chicken stock
- 1 onion, chopped
- 30 oz. pumpkin purée
- 2 cups chopped sweet potato
- Salt and pepper, to taste
- Sour cream, for serving

Directions:

1. Add all the ingredients, except for the sour cream, in the Instant Pot.
2. Lock the lid. Select the Manual mode, then set the timer for 8 minutes at High Pressure.
3. Once the timer goes off, do a quick pressure release. Carefully open the lid.
4. Transfer the soup into a blender and pulse until smooth.
5. Serve with sour cream on top.

Sage Zucchini Soup

Serves:4 | Cooking Time: 15 Minutes

Ingredients:

- 1 lb zucchini, cut into strips
- 1 tbsp dried sage
- ½ tsp garlic powder
- Salt and black pepper to taste
- 1 tsp olive oil
- 4 cups vegetable broth

Directions:

1. Place zucchini in a large bowl. Add sage, olive oil,

salt, pepper, and garlic, and mix to coat thoroughly. Pour broth into the IP and add in the zucchini mixture. Seal the lid and cook for 3 minutes on Manual at High. Do a quick release and serve.

Potato Soup

Serves: 8 | Cooking Time: 15 Minutes

Ingredients:

- 3 lbs. potatoes, peeled and cubed
- 2 cups milk
- ¼ tsp. salt
- 12 green onions, chopped
- 1 cup shredded Cheddar cheese

Directions:

1. In the Instant Pot, mix the potatoes with milk and salt. Stir to combine.
2. Lock the lid. Select the Manual mode and set the timer for 12 minutes at High Pressure.
3. Once the timer goes off, do a quick pressure release. Carefully open the lid.
4. Add the Cheddar cheese and green onions, and stir to mix well.
5. Set the pot to Sauté and cook until the cheese melts, about 3 minutes.
6. Ladle the soup into bowls and serve.

Black Chicken Stew

Serves:4 | Cooking Time: 30 Minutes

Ingredients:

- 2 tbsp mixed berries
- 3 slices of fresh ginger
- A handful of walnuts
- A handful of dates
- Salt and black pepper to taste
- 1 (3.5-oz) whole black chicken

Directions:

1. Clean the insides of the chicken. Add ½ cup water to your IP. In a mixing bowl, mix all the ingredients together with your hands. Stuff the mixture into the chicken and place in the cooker. Season with salt and pepper. Seal the lid, select Manual at High, and cook for 20 minutes. When ready, release the pressure naturally for 5 minutes. Remove the chicken from the pot. Slice and place on Serves: plates.

Coconut Seafood Soup

Serves: 5 | Cooking Time: 8 Minutes

Ingredients:

- 1 cup coconut milk
- 10 shrimps, shelled and deveined
- 1 thumb-size ginger, crushed
- 4 tilapia fillets
- 2 cups water
- Salt and pepper, to taste

Directions:

1. Place all ingredients in the Instant Pot. Stir to combine well.
2. Lock the lid. Set on the Manual mode, then set the timer to 8 minutes at Low Pressure.
3. When the timer goes off, perform a quick release.
4. Carefully open the lid. Allow to cool before serving.

Cheesy Broccoli Soup

Serves: 8 | Cooking Time: 10 Minutes

Ingredients:

- 4 garlic cloves, minced
- 4 cups broccoli florets
- 3½ cups chicken stock
- 1 cup heavy whipping cream
- Salt and pepper, to taste
- 3 cups grated Cheddar cheese

Directions:

1. Set the Instant Pot to Sauté, then add the garlic and sauté it for 1 minute until fragrant.
2. Add the broccoli, stock and cream. Sprinkle with salt and pepper. Stir to combine well.
3. Lock the lid. Select the Manual mode, then set the timer for 8 to 9 minutes at Low Pressure.
4. Once the timer goes off, do a quick pressure release.
5. Carefully open the lid. Add the cheese and stir until it melts, then ladle into bowls and serve.

Thai Coconut Shrimp Soup

Serves: 2 | Cooking Time: 6 Minutes

Ingredients:

- 6 oz. shrimps, shelled and deveined
- 2 cups water
- Juice of 3 kaffir limes
- 1½ cups coconut milk
- 1 cup fresh cilantro

Directions:

1. In the Instant Pot, add all the ingredients excluding cilantro.
2. Lock the lid. Set on the Manual mode and set the timer to 6 minutes at Low Pressure.
3. When the timer goes off, perform a quick release.
4. Carefully open the lid. Garnish with the fresh cilantro and serve immediately.

Leftover Chicken Soup

Serves: 3 | Cooking Time: 12 Minutes

Ingredients:

- 1 tbsp. coconut oil
- 1 onion, chopped
- 8 garlic cloves, minced
- 2 cups shredded leftover chicken meat
- Salt and pepper, to taste
- 7 cups water

Directions:

1. Press the Sauté button on the Instant Pot and heat the coconut oil.
2. Sauté the onions and garlic for 2 to 3 minutes until fragrant.
3. Add the chicken meat and sprinkle salt and pepper for seasoning.
4. Pour in the water. Season with more salt and pepper.
5. Lock the lid. Set on the Manual mode, then set the timer to 10 minutes at High Pressure.
6. When the timer goes off, do a natural pressure release for 10 minutes, then release any remaining pressure.
7. Carefully open the lid and serve warm.

Chili Con Carne (chili With Meat)

Serves: 2 | Cooking Time: 35 Minutes

Ingredients:

- 2 cups chopped tomatoes
- 3 tbsps. mixed seasoning
- 1lb. ground beef
- 3 squares dark chocolate
- 1 cup mixed beans

Directions:

1. Mix all the ingredients in the Instant Pot.
2. Lock the lid. Select the Meat/Stew setting. Set the timer for 35 minutes at High Pressure.
3. Once cooking is complete, perform a natural pressure release for 10 minutes, then release any remaining pressure. Carefully open the lid.
4. Serve warm.

Broccoli Cheddar Soup

Serves: 4 | Cooking Time: 10 Minutes

Ingredients:

- 2 heads fresh broccoli
- 4 cups chicken broth
- 1 cup heavy whipping cream
- Salt and pepper, to taste
- 2 cups shredded Cheddar cheese
- Add the trivet to the bottom of the Instant Pot along with broccoli and broth.
- Lock the lid. Select the Manual mode, then set the timer for 10 minutes at High Pressure.
- Once the timer goes off, do a quick pressure release. Carefully open the lid.
- Remove the trivet and add the cream, salt and pepper. Whisk well.
- Purée the soup with an immersion blender.
- Add the cheese to the soup and keep stirring until melted.
- Ladle into bowls and serve.

Snacks & Desserts , Appetizers Recipes

Snacks & Desserts , Appetizers Recipes

Parmesan Asparagus

Servings: 4 | Cooking Time: 15 Minutes

Ingredients:

- 2 tbsp butter, softened
- 1 lb asparagus, chopped
- 2 garlic cloves, minced
- Salt and black pepper to taste
- 2 tbsp grated Parmesan cheese

Directions:

1. In your Instant Pot, place 1 cup of water and a trivet. Cut out a foil sheet, place asparagus on top as well as garlic and butter. Season with salt and pepper. Wrap foil and place asparagus packet on the trivet. Seal the lid, select Pressure Cook on High, and set the time to 8 minutes. When ready, do a quick pressure release. Remove foil pack, put asparagus onto a platter, and top with Parmesan cheese to serve.

Delicious Dulce De Leche

Serves: 2 | Cooking Time: 35 Minutes

Ingredients:

- 1 can (14-ounce sweetened condensed milk

Directions:

1. Place a trivet and steamer basket in the inner pot. Place the can of milk in the steamer basket.
2. Add water until the can is covered.
3. Secure the lid. Choose the "Manual" mode and cook for 20 minutes at High pressure. Once cooking is complete, use a natural pressure release for 10 minutes; carefully remove the lid.
4. Don't open the can until it is completely cooled. Bon appétit!

Cumin Dip

Serves: 4 | Cooking Time: 2 Minutes

Ingredients:

- 1 tbsp. hot sauce
- 1 tbsp. lime juice
- 1 cup sour cream
- 1¼ tsps. ground cumin
- ⅓ cup mayonnaise

Directions:

1. In the Instant Pot, mix sour cream with cumin and hot sauce, and stir to combine well.
2. Lock the lid. Select the Manual mode, then set the timer for 2 minutes at High Pressure.
3. Once the timer goes off, do a quick pressure release. Carefully open the lid.
4. Allow the dip to rest until cooled completely. Add the mayo and lime juice and stir well, then serve.

Raspberry Curd

Serves: 6-8 | Cooking Time: 30 Minutes

Ingredients:

- 18 oz raspberries
- 1½ cups sugar
- 3 tbsp lemon juice
- 3 egg yolks
- 3 tbsp butter

Directions:

1. In the Instant Pot, combine the raspberries, sugar and lemon juice.
2. Close and lock the lid. Select the MANUAL setting and set the cooking time for 2 minutes at HIGH pressure.
3. When the timer goes off, let the pressure Release Naturally for 5 minutes, then release any remaining steam manually. Open the lid.
4. Use the mesh strainer to puree the raspberries and remove the seeds.
5. In a bowl, whisk egg yolks and combine with the raspberries puree.
6. Return the mixture to the pot. Select SAUTÉ and bring the mixture to a boil, stirring constantly.
7. Press the CANCEL key to stop the SAUTÉ function.
8. Add the butter and stir to combine.
9. Serve chilled.

Creamy Avocado Spread

Serves: 4 | Cooking Time: 2 Minutes

Ingredients:

- 1 cup coconut milk
- 2 pitted, peeled and halved avocados
- Juice of 2 limes
- ½ cup chopped cilantro
- ¼ tsp. stevia
- 1 cup water

Directions:

1. In the Instant Pot, add the water and steamer basket. Place the avocados in the basket.
2. Lock the lid. Select the Manual mode and set the cooking time for 2 minutes at High Pressure.
3. Once cooking is complete, do a quick pressure release. Carefully open the lid.
4. Transfer the avocados to your blender, and add the cilantro, stevia, lime juice, and coconut milk, and blend, or until it reaches your desired consistency. Serve immediately or refrigerate to chill until ready to use.

Southern Peanuts

Serves: 4 | Cooking Time: 1 Hour 15 Minutes

Ingredients:

- 1 lb. peanuts
- ¼ cup sea salt
- 1 tbsp. Cajun seasoning
- 2 garlic cloves, minced
- 1 jalapeño pepper, chopped

Directions:

1. In the Instant Pot mix peanuts with sea salt, Cajun seasoning, garlic and jalapeño.
2. Add enough water to cover.
3. Lock the lid. Select the Manual mode, then set the timer for 1 hour and 15 minutes at High Pressure.
4. Once the timer goes off, do a quick pressure release. Carefully open the lid.
5. Drain the peanuts and transfer to bowls, then serve.

Sesame Crispy Asparagus

Servings:x | Cooking Time: 10 Minutes

Ingredients:

- 1 pound fresh asparagus, trimmed
- 1 tablespoon sesame oil
- 2 tablespoons sesame seeds, toasted
- 1 teaspoon garlic powder
- Kosher salt and red pepper, to taste

Directions:

1. Add 1 cup of water and a steamer basket to the inner pot. Place the asparagus in the steamer basket.
2. Secure the lid. Choose the "Steam" mode and cook for 3 minutes at High pressure. Once cooking is complete, use a quick pressure release; carefully remove the lid.
3. Toss the warm asparagus with the other ingredients. Enjoy!

Simple Cake Bars

Serves: 12 | Cooking Time: 20 Minutes

Ingredients:

- 1 yellow cake mix
- ½ cup milk
- 1 egg, whisked
- ⅓ cup canola oil
- 1 cup baking chips
- 1½ cups water

Directions:

1. In a bowl, mix cake mix with milk, eggs, oil and baking chips, stir well, pour into a baking pan and spread well.
2. Add the water to the Instant Pot, add trivet, add baking pan inside.
3. Lock the lid. Set the Instant Pot to Manual mode, then set the timer for 20 minutes at High Pressure.
4. When the timer goes off, perform a natural release for 8 to 10 minutes. Carefully open the lid.
5. Leave cake to cool down, cut into medium bars and serve.

Flavored Pears

Serves: 4 | Cooking Time: 10 Minutes

Ingredients:

- 11 oz. currant jelly
- 26 oz. grape juice
- Juice and zest of 1 lemon
- 4 pears
- 2 rosemary springs

Directions:

1. Transfer the currant jelly and grape juice to the Instant Pot and add lemon zest and juice before stirring.
2. Add pears and rosemary springs.
3. Lock the lid. Set the Instant Pot to Manual mode, then set the timer for 10 minutes at High Pressure.
4. When the timer goes off, perform a quick release. Carefully open the lid.
5. Arrange pears on plates and serve them cold with the cooking juice on top.

Zucchini Spread

Serves: 6 | Cooking Time: 9 Minutes

Ingredients:

- ½ cup water
- 1 tbsp. olive oil
- 1 bunch basil, chopped
- 1½ lbs. zucchinis, chopped
- 2 garlic cloves, minced

Directions:

1. Set the Instant Pot to Sauté and heat the olive oil. Cook the garlic cloves for 3 minutes, stirring occasionally.
2. Add zucchinis and water, and mix well.
3. Lock the lid. Select the Manual mode, then set the timer for 3 minutes at High Pressure.
4. Once the timer goes off, do a quick pressure release. Carefully open the lid.
5. Add the basil and blend the mixture with an immersion blender until smooth.
6. Select the Simmer mode and cook for 2 minutes more.
7. Transfer to a bowl and serve warm.

Kale And Wild Rice Appetizer Salad

Serves: 4 | Cooking Time: 25 Minutes

Ingredients:

- 1 tsp. olive oil
- 1 avocado, peeled, pitted and chopped
- 3 oz. goat cheese, crumbled
- 1 cup cooked wild rice
- 1 bunch kale, roughly chopped

Directions:

1. Set the Instant Pot to Sauté and heat the olive oil.
2. Add the rice and toast for 2 to 3 minutes, stirring often.
3. Add kale and stir well.
4. Lock the lid. Select the Manual mode, then set the timer for 20 minutes at Low Pressure.
5. Once the timer goes off, do a natural pressure release for 10 minutes, then release any remaining pressure. Carefully open the lid.
6. Add avocado and toss well. Sprinkle the cheese on top and serve.

Butternut And Coconut Pudding

Servings:x | Cooking Time: 20 Minutes

Ingredients:

- 3/4 pound butternut squash, peeled, seeded, and diced
- 1/2 cup coconut cream
- 3 tablespoons maple syrup
- A pinch of kosher salt
- 1/2 teaspoon pumpkin pie spice mix
- 2 tablespoons almond milk

Directions:

1. Add 1 cup of water and a metal rack to the bottom of the inner pot. Place your squash in a steamer basket; lower the basket onto the rack.
2. Secure the lid. Choose the "Steam" mode and cook for 10 minutes at High pressure. Once cooking is complete, use a quick pressure release; carefully remove the lid.
3. Stir the remaining ingredients into the cooked squash; combine all ingredients with a potato masher.
4. Let it cook on the "Sauté" function until everything is thoroughly heated or about 4 minutes. Serve immediately.

Basil-mascarpone & Blue Cheese Sauce

Servings: 4 | Cooking Time: 15 Minutes

Ingredients:

- 2 tbsp butter
- 1 cup heavy cream
- 1 ½ cups mascarpone cheese
- 1 cup crumbled blue cheese
- 1 tsp dried basil
- Salt and black pepper to taste

Directions:

1. Select Sauté and boil heavy cream until thickened, while occasionally stirring. Whisk in mascarpone cheese, blue cheese, and butter to melt for 2 minutes. Stir in basil, salt, and pepper. Press Cancel. Spoon sauce into serving cups.

Jamaican Hibiscus Tea

Servings:x | Cooking Time: 20 Minutes

Ingredients:

- 2 cups water
- 1/4 cup dried hibiscus flowers
- 1/4 cup brown sugar
- 1/2 teaspoon fresh ginger, peeled and minced
- 1 tablespoon lime juice

Directions:

1. Combine all ingredients, except for the lime juice, in the inner pot of your Instant Pot.
2. Secure the lid. Choose the "Manual" mode and cook for 5 minutes at High pressure. Once cooking is complete, use a natural pressure release for 10 minutes; carefully remove the lid.
3. Stir in the lime juice and serve well chilled.

Tapioca Pudding

Serves: 2-4 | Cooking Time: 20 Minutes

Ingredients:

- 1½ cups water
- 1/3 cup tapioca pearls
- 1¼ cups whole milk
- ½ cup sugar
- 1 tsp lemon zest

Directions:

1. Pour the water into the Instant Pot and set a steam rack in the pot.
2. In a baking dish that can fit into the pot, combine the tapioca, milk, sugar and lemon zest.
3. Place the baking dish on the rack. Close and lock the lid.
4. Select MANUAL and cook at HIGH pressure for 10 minutes.
5. When the timer beeps, use a Quick Release. Carefully unlock the lid.
6. Serve.

Authentic Spanish Crema Catalana

Serves:4 | Cooking Time: 15 Minutes

Ingredients:

- ½ tsp vanilla paste
- ½ tsp cinnamon extract
- 1 ½ cups warm heavy cream
- 3 large-sized egg yolks
- 1 cup sugar

Directions:

1. In a bowl, mix cinnamon, heavy cream, sugar and egg yolks. Fill 4 ramekins with this mixture and wrap with foil. Pour 1 cup of water into the IP. Add a trivet and lay the ramekins on top. Seal the lid, press Manual, and cook for 10 minutes at High. Once the cooking is over, do a quick pressure release. Refrigerate Crema Catalana for at least 2 hours.

Mexican Thickened Hot Chocolate (champurrado)

Servings:6 | Cooking Time: 35 Minutes

Ingredients:

- 3 cups whole milk
- ½ cup masa harina
- 3 cups water
- 1 bar Mexican chocolate, cut into 8 pieces
- 1 cinnamon stick, plus more for garnish
- ½ cup sugar, divided

Directions:

1. In a blender, combine the milk, masa harina, and water and puree until smooth. Pour into the inner pot and add the chocolate, cinnamon stick, and ¼ cup of the sugar. Stir until the sugar has completely dissolved.

2. Lock the lid into place. Select Pressure Cook or Manual; set the pressure to High and the time to 8 minutes.

3. After the cook time is complete, let the pressure release Naturally. Unlock and remove the lid. Discard the cinnamon stick.

4. Stir the champurrado gently to combine. Sweeten with the remaining ¼ cup sugar, if desired. Ladle into mugs. Garnish with cinnamon sticks.

Brussels Sprouts With Balsamic Vinegar

Servings:4 | Cooking Time: 30 Minutes

Ingredients:

- 25 Brussels sprouts, halved lengthwise
- 1 tablespoon extra-virgin olive oil
- 2 garlic cloves, minced
- 1 tablespoon balsamic vinegar
- 1 teaspoon kosher salt
- ½ teaspoon freshly ground black pepper
- 1 tablespoon toasted sesame seeds

Directions:

1. Pour 1 cup water into the inner pot. Place the Brussel sprouts in a steamer basket and place the basket in the pot.

2. Lock the lid into place. Select Steam; set the pressure to High and the time to 1 minute.

3. After the cook time is complete, Quick release the pressure. Unlock and remove the lid. Using tongs, carefully remove the steamer basket. Discard the water from the inner pot, wipe it dry, and return the pot to the base.

4. Select Sauté, set the heat to Medium, and add the olive oil. When the oil shimmers, add the garlic and sauté for 1 minute. Add the Brussels sprouts, vinegar, salt, and pepper and sauté for 2 minutes. Sprinkle with the sesame seeds and serve hot.

Caramel Corns

Servings: 4 | Cooking Time: 15 Minutes

Ingredients:

- 4 tbsp butter
- 1 cup sweet corn kernels
- 3 tbsp brown sugar
- ¼ cup whole milk

Directions:

1. Set your Instant Pot to Sauté, melt butter, and mix in corn kernels. Once heated and popping, cover the top with a clear instant pot safe lid, and continue cooking until corn stops popping for 3 minutes.

2. Open the lid and transfer popcorns to a bowl. Press Cancel and wipe the inner pot clean. Select Sauté. Combine in brown sugar and milk and cook with frequent stirring until sugar dissolves and sauce coats the back of the spoon, 3-4 minutes. Turn Instant Pot off. Drizzle caramel sauce all over corns and toss to coat thoroughly. Cool and serve.

Easiest Mashed Potatoes

Servings:4 | Cooking Time: 25 Minutes

Ingredients:

- 2 pounds russet potatoes, peeled and cut into 1- to 2-inch chunks
- 1 teaspoon kosher salt, plus more to taste
- 1½ cups whole milk
- ½ cup heavy (whipping) cream
- 3 tablespoons unsalted butter
- ¼ teaspoon freshly ground black pepper

Directions:

1. Put the potatoes in the inner pot and sprinkle them with the salt. Add the milk, cream, and butter.

2. Lock the lid into place. Select Pressure Cook or Manual; set the pressure to High and the time to 8 minutes.

3. After the cook time is complete, Quick release the pressure. Unlock and remove the lid.

4. Using a potato masher or large fork, mash the potatoes into the milk mixture until smooth and creamy. (Alternatively, you can remove the potatoes with a slotted spoon or skimmer and use a ricer to press the potatoes into the pot, then stir to combine them with the milk mixture.) Season with the pepper and additional salt, if necessary, and serve.

Classic Hummus Dip

Servings:x | Cooking Time: 45 Minutes | Servings 8

Ingredients:

- 1 tablespoon olive oil
- 1 yellow onion, chopped
- 2 garlic cloves, minced
- 1 ½ cups dried chickpeas
- 4 cups water
- 3 tablespoons tahini paste
- 2 tablespoons fresh lemon juice

Directions:

1. Press the "Sauté" button to preheat your Instant Pot. Once hot, heat the olive oil until sizzling. Then, cook the onion and garlic until tender and fragrant; reserve.
2. Wipe down the Instant Pot with a damp cloth. Then, add chickpeas and water to the Instant Pot.
3. Secure the lid and choose the "Bean/Chili" function; cook for 40 minutes at High pressure. Once cooking is complete, use a natural release; carefully remove the lid.
4. Drain chickpeas, reserving cooking liquid. Now, transfer chickpeas to your blender. Add tahini, lemon juice, and reserved onion/garlic mixture.
5. Process until everything is creamy, uniform, and smooth, adding a splash of cooking liquid. Serve with pita bread and vegetable sticks.

Chocolate Fondue

Serves: 3-6 | Cooking Time: 25 Minutes

Ingredients:

- One 100 g bar dark chocolate 70-85%, cut into large chunks
- 1 tbsp sugar
- 1 tsp amaretto liqueur
- ½ cup heavy cream
- 2 cups water

Directions:

1. Divide the chocolate, sugar, amaretto liqueur, and heavy cream between 3 ramekins.
2. Pour the water into the Instant Pot and set a steam rack in the pot.
3. Place the ramekins on the rack. Close and lock the lid.
4. Select MANUAL and cook at HIGH pressure for 3 minutes.
5. When cooking is complete, let the pressure Release

Naturally for 10 minutes. Release any remaining steam manually. Uncover the pot.
6. Remove the ramekins from the pot.
7. Using a fork quickly stir the contents of the ramekins vigorously for about 1 minute, until the texture is smooth and thick.
8. Serve with fresh fruit or bread pieces.

Spicy Kale

Servings:4 | Cooking Time: 25 Minutes

Ingredients:

- 1 tablespoon extra-virgin olive oil
- 2 garlic cloves, minced
- 1 kale bunch, leaves stemmed and chopped
- 1 cup water
- 1 tablespoon red wine vinegar
- ½ teaspoon red pepper flakes
- ¼ teaspoon kosher salt

Directions:

1. Select Sauté, set the heat to Medium, and add the olive oil. When the oil shimmers, add the garlic and sauté for 30 seconds, stirring continuously. Add the kale and water to the pot.
2. Lock the lid into place. Select Pressure Cook or Manual; set the pressure to High and the time to 5 minutes.
3. After the cook time is complete, Quick release the pressure. Unlock and remove the lid.
4. Toss the cooked kale with the vinegar, red pepper flakes, and salt. Serve hot.

Blackberry Yogurt Jars

Servings: 4 | Cooking Time: 8 Hrs 20 Min + Cooling Time

Ingredients:

- 8 cups whole milk
- ½ cup plain yogurt
- 2 tbsp vanilla bean paste
- 1 cup blackberries

Directions:

1. Pour milk into your Instant Pot. Seal the lid, select Yogurt, and press Adjust until the display shows "Boil." When done, press Cancel and unlock the lid. Stir the milk, remove the pot, and allow cooling up to 100°F. Check the temperature with a food thermometer.
2. Whisk in yogurt and vanilla bean paste. Return

the inner pot to Instant Pot. Seal the lid, select Yogurt mode, and set the cooking time to 8 hours. After cooking, the display will show "Yogt." Refrigerate the yogurt for a few hours.

3. Mash the blackberries in a bowl using a fork. Divide them between mason jars and top with yogurt. Serve.

Caribbean Hot Sauce

Servings: 4 | Cooking Time: 20 Minutes

Ingredients:
- 8 cups habanero peppers, heads removed
- 3 tbsp salt
- 1 ¼ cups water
- 6 garlic cloves, crushed
- ¼ cup tequila
- ¼ cup agave nectar
- ¼ cup apple cider vinegar

Directions:

1. Add habanero peppers, salt, water, and garlic to the inner pot. Seal the lid, select Pressure Cook on High, and set to 2 minutes. After cooking, allow a natural release for 10 minutes. Stir in tequila, agave nectar, and vinegar. Using an immersion blender, process ingredients until smooth. Spoon into jars and refrigerate. Use for up to 2 months.

Strawberry And Chia Marmalade

Serves: 6 | Cooking Time: 4 Minutes

Ingredients:
- 4 tbsps. sugar
- 2 tbsps. chia seeds
- 2 lbs. halved strawberries
- Zest of 1 grated lemon
- ½ tsp. vanilla extract

Directions:

1. In the Instant Pot, mix sugar with strawberries, vanilla extract, lemon zest and chia seeds, stir.
2. Lock the lid. Set the Instant Pot to Manual mode, then set the timer for 4 minutes at High Pressure.
3. When the timer goes off, perform a natural release. Carefully open the lid.
4. Stir again, divide into cups and serve cold

Cashew Spread

Serves: 8 | Cooking Time: 6 Minutes

Ingredients:
- ¼ cup nutritional yeast
- ¼ tsp. garlic powder
- ½ cup soaked and drained cashews
- 10 oz. hummus
- ½ cup water

Directions:

1. In the Instant Pot, combine the cashews and water.
2. Lock the lid. Select the Manual mode, then set the timer for 6 minutes at High Pressure.
3. Once the timer goes off, do a quick pressure release. Carefully open the lid.
4. Transfer the cashews to the blender, and add hummus, yeast and garlic powder, and pulse until well combined. Serve immediately.

Cinnamon Yogurt Custard

Servings:4 | Cooking Time: 1 Hour

Ingredients:
- ½ cup plain Greek yogurt
- ½ cup sweetened condensed milk
- ½ teaspoon ground cinnamon
- ¼ cup chopped fruit or berries of your choice, for garnish

Directions:

1. Place the trivet in the inner pot, then pour in 1 cup water.
2. In a heatproof bowl that fits inside the Instant Pot, mix together the yogurt, condensed milk, and cinnamon. Tightly cover the bowl with aluminum foil. Place the bowl on the trivet.
3. Lock the lid into place. Select Pressure Cook or Manual; set the pressure to High and the time to 25 minutes.
4. After the cook time is complete, let the pressure release Naturally. Unlock and remove the lid. Carefully remove the bowl. Let it cool at room temperature for 30 minutes, then refrigerate, covered, for 3 hours.
5. Serve garnished with the fruits of your choice.

Hard-boiled Eggs With Paprika

Serves: 5 | Cooking Time: 20 Minutes

Ingredients:

- 1 cup water
- 5 large eggs
- Salt and black pepper, to taste
- A pinch of paprika

Directions:

1. In the pot, add water and place a trivet. Lay your eggs on top. Seal the lid and cook for 5 minutes on High Pressure. Do a natural release for 10 minutes. Transfer the eggs to ice cold water to cool completely. Peel and season with paprika, salt and pepper before serving.

Greek-style Dipping Sauce

Servings:x | Cooking Time: 20 Minutes

Ingredients:

- 1 artichoke
- 2 tablespoons mayonnaise
- 2 tablespoons Greek yogurt
- 1 teaspoon Dijon mustard
- 1/2 teaspoon tzatziki spice mix

Directions:

1. Place 1 cup of water and a steamer basket in the inner pot of your Instant Pot.
2. Place the artichokes in the steamer basket.
3. Secure the lid. Choose the "Manual" mode and cook for 11 minutes at High pressure. Once cooking is complete, use a quick pressure release; carefully remove the lid.
4. Meanwhile, whisk the remaining ingredients to prepare the sauce. Serve the artichokes with the Greek sauce on the side. Bon appétit!

Greek Meatballs

Serves: 10 | Cooking Time: 12 Minutes

Ingredients:

- 1 egg, whisked
- ¼ cup chopped mint
- 1 lb. ground beef
- 3 tbsps. olive oil
- ¼ cup white vinegar

Directions:

1. In a bowl, mix the beef with mint and egg, and whisk well. Shape the beef mixture into 10 meatballs with your hands.
2. Set the Instant Pot to Sauté and heat the olive oil.
3. Add the beef meatballs and brown them for about 4 minutes on each side.
4. Add the vinegar and stir to mix well.
5. Lock the lid. Select the Manual mode, then set the timer for 4 minutes at High Pressure.
6. Once the timer goes off, do a quick pressure release. Carefully open the lid.
7. Divide the meatballs among plates and serve them with a yogurt dip on the side.

Quick Coconut Treat With Pears

Serves: 2 | Cooking Time: 15 Minutes

Ingredients:

- ¼ cup flour
- 1 cup coconut milk
- 2 pears, peeled and diced
- ¼ cup shredded coconut, unsweetened

Directions:

1. Combine all ingredients in your Pressure cooker. Seal the lid, select Pressure Cook and set the timer to 5 minutes at High pressure. When ready, do a quick pressure release. Divide the mixture between two bowls.

Sweet Orange Balls

Serves:20 | Cooking Time: 10 Minutes

Ingredients:

- 2 ½ cups sugar
- 3 tbsp orange juice
- 6 cups milk
- 1 tsp ground cardamom

Directions:

1. Press Sauté on your IP and add milk. Bring to a boil and stir in orange juice. Pour milk through a cheesecloth-lined colander. Drain as much liquid as you can. Place the obtained paneer on a smooth surface. Form a ball and divide it into 20 equal pieces. Pour 6 cups of water and bring to a boil. Add sugar and cardamom and cook until dissolved. Shape the dumplings into balls, and place them in the syrup. Seal the lid and cook for 5 minutes on Manual at High. Once done, do a quick pressure release. Let cool for at least 2 hours.

Pumpkin Pie Cups

Servings:4 | Cooking Time: 30 Minutes

Ingredients:

- 1 cup canned pure pumpkin puree
- 1 cup nondairy milk
- 6 tablespoons unrefined (crystallized) sugar (less if using sweetened milk), plus more for sprinkling
- ¼ cup spelt flour or all-purpose flour
- ½ teaspoon pumpkin pie spice
- Pinch kosher salt

Directions:

1. Place the trivet in the inner pot, then pour in 1 cup water.
2. In a medium bowl, stir together the pumpkin, milk, sugar, flour, pumpkin pie spice, and salt. Pour the mixture into four heatproof small ramekins or custard cups. Sprinkle a bit more sugar on the top of each, if you like. Cover the ramekins with aluminum foil, then place them on the trivet, stacking them if needed (three on the bottom, one on top).
3. Lock the lid into place. Select Pressure Cook or Manual; set the pressure to High and the time to 6 minutes.
4. After the cook time is complete, Quick release the pressure. Unlock and remove the lid. Let cool for a few minutes before carefully lifting out the ramekins with oven mitts or tongs.
5. Let cool for at least 10 minutes before serving.

Buttery Steamed Sweet Potatoes

Servings:4 | Cooking Time: 35 Minutes

Ingredients:

- 1 pound whole small sweet potatoes, cleaned
- 1/4 teaspoon salt
- 1/4 teaspoon freshly grated nutmeg
- 2 tablespoons light butter

Directions:

1. Add 1 cup of water and a steamer basket to the Instant Pot. Arrange sweet potatoes in the steamer basket.
2. Secure the lid and choose the "Steam" mode. Cook for 10 minutes under High pressure. Once cooking is complete, use a natural release for 20 minutes; carefully remove the lid.
3. Toss steamed sweet potatoes with salt, nutmeg and butter. Eat warm. Bon appétit!

Lemon Marmalade

Serves: 4-6 Jars | Cooking Time: 30 Minutes

Ingredients:

- 1 lb lemons, quartered, deseeded, and sliced with a mandolin
- ½ cup water
- 2 lbs sugar

Directions:

1. Add the lemons and water to the Instant Pot.
2. Close and lock the lid. Select MANUAL and cook at HIGH pressure for 10 minutes.
3. When the timer beeps, use a Natural Release for 10 minutes. Uncover the pot.
4. Add the sugar and stir for 2 minutes until the sugar melts.
5. Select SAUTÉ and bring to a boil, cook for 5 minutes.
6. Transfer the mixture into clean or sterilized jars.
7. Serve chilled or store in the refrigerator.

Barbecue Corn With Potato Chips

Servings:4 | Cooking Time: 10 Minutes

Ingredients:

- 4 ears corn on the cob, husks removed
- 1/3 cup barbecue sauce
- 1/2 cup potato chips, crushed

Directions:

1. Add water and metal trivet to the base of your Instant Pot. Place ears corn on the cob on a metal trivet.
2. Secure the lid. Choose the "Steam" mode and cook for 2 minutes under High pressure. Once cooking is complete, use a quick release; carefully remove the lid.
3. Brush each corn on the cob with barbecue sauce; sprinkle with crushed chips. Bon appétit!

Movie Night Almond Popcorn

Servings:4 | Cooking Time: 10 Minutes

Ingredients:

- 3 tablespoons butter, at room temperature
- 1/4 cup popcorn kernels
- A pinch of sugar
- Sea salt, to taste
- 2 tablespoons Habanero BBQ almonds

Directions:

1. Press the "Sauté" button to heat up the Instant Pot. Melt the butter until sizzling.
2. Stir in popcorn kernels; stir until they are covered with melted butter.
3. Once popcorn starts popping, cover with the lid. Shake for a few seconds.
4. Now, turn off the Instant Pot when 2/3 of kernels have popped. Allow all kernels to pop.
5. Add salt and Habanero BBQ almonds; toss and serve immediately. Enjoy!

Colby Spinach & Asparagus Dip

Serves:16 | Cooking Time: 20 Minutes

Ingredients:

- 18 oz asparagus, chopped
- 12 oz spinach, chopped
- 1 ½ cups Colby, shredded
- Salt and black pepper to taste
- ½ cup mayonnaise
- 1 cup half-and-half

Directions:

1. Insert a trivet in the IP and pour 1 cup of water. In a baking dish, add all ingredients and stir well. Cover with aluminium foil and lower on top of the trivet. Seal the lid and cook for 12 minutes on Manual at High. Do a quick release, and serve with crackers.

Steamed Spicy And Cheesy Potatoes

Servings:x | Cooking Time: 30 Minutes

Ingredients:

- 2 medium potatoes, peeled
- 1/4 cup cream cheese
- 2 tablespoons salsa

Directions:

1. Place 1 cup of water and a metal trivet in the inner pot of your Instant Pot. Pierce your potatoes with a fork; place them on the trivet.
2. Secure the lid. Choose the "Steam" mode and cook for 15 minutes at High pressure. Once cooking is complete, use a natural pressure release for 10 minutes; carefully remove the lid.
3. Top the warm potatoes with the cream cheese and salsa and serve immediately. Bon appétit!

Chicken Dip

Serves: 6 | Cooking Time: 15 Minutes

Ingredients:

- 1 cup Greek yogurt
- 4 oz. cream cheese
- ½ cup hot sauce
- 3 cups cooked and shredded chicken
- 1 cup shredded Mozzarella cheese

Directions:

1. In the Instant Pot, mix chicken with cream cheese and hot sauce, and stir to combine well.
2. Lock the lid. Select the Manual mode, then set the timer for 15 minutes at High Pressure.
3. Once the timer goes off, do a natural pressure release for 10 minutes, then release any remaining pressure. Carefully open the lid.
4. Add the yogurt and Mozzarella cheese. Give the mixture a good stir. Let rest for about 8 minutes, then serve.

Honey-glazed Carrots

Servings: 4 | Cooking Time: 15 Minutes

Ingredients:

- ¼ cup butter, melted
- 3 large carrots, cut into chunks
- 1 cup vegetable stock
- 2 tbsp honey
- 1 tbsp chopped parsley
- Salt and black pepper to taste

Directions:

1. Add carrots, vegetable stock, salt, and pepper to your Instant Pot. Seal the lid, select Pressure Cook on High, and set the time to 2 minutes. After cooking, do a quick pressure release. Using a slotted spoon, fetch out carrots into a baking sheet. Brush with butter and honey and cook under the broiler for 4 minutes. Top with parsley and serve.

White Chocolate-milk Faux Muffins

Servings: 4 | Cooking Time: 15 Minutes

Ingredients:

- 1 white chocolate chip, melted
- ½ cup whole milk

Directions:

1. In a medium bowl, mix white chocolate with milk until well combined. Lightly grease a silicone egg bite tray with cooking spray and fill with chocolate mixture two-thirds way up. Cover egg tray loosely with foil.
2. Pour 1 cup of water into your Instant Pot, fit in a trivet, and place egg bite tray on top. Seal the lid, select Manual/Pressure Cook on High, and set time to 12 minutes. After cooking, perform a quick pressure release to let out steam, and unlock the lid. Carefully remove the tray, take off the foil, allow cooling for 5 minutes, and pop out dessert bites.

Green Olive Pâté

Serves: 4 | Cooking Time: 2 Minutes

Ingredients:

- ½ cup olive oil
- 2 anchovy fillets
- 1 tbsp. chopped capers
- 2 cups pitted green olives
- 2 garlic cloves, minced

Directions:

1. In a food processor, process the olives with anchovy fillets, garlic, capers and olive oil, then transfer to the Instant Pot.
2. Lock the lid. Select the Manual mode, then set the timer for 2 minutes at Low Pressure.
3. Once the timer goes off, do a quick pressure release. Carefully open the lid.
4. Remove from the pot and serve warm.

White Chocolate Mousse

Serves: 6 | Cooking Time: 3 Minutes

Ingredients:

- 12 oz. chopped white chocolate
- 12 oz. chopped black chocolate
- 2 cups heavy cream
- 1 tbsp. sugar
- 1 tsp. vanilla extract

Directions:

1. In the Instant Pot, mix white and black chocolate with cream. Stir to combine well.
2. Lock the lid. Set the Instant Pot to Manual mode, then set the timer for 3 minutes at High Pressure.
3. When the timer goes off, perform a quick release. Carefully open the lid.
4. Add the sugar and vanilla, stir until the sugar melts, divide into bowls and serve cold.

Asian Coconut Rice Pudding

Serves: 8 | Cooking Time: 10 Minutes

Ingredients:

- 1 ½ cups sticky rice
- ¾ cup sugar
- ½ teaspoon salt
- 3 cups coconut milk
- 1 stalk pandan leaf

Directions:

1. Put everything in the Instant Pot.
2. Give a good stir.
3. Close the lid and press the Rice button.
4. Adjust the cooking time to 10 minutes.
5. Do natural pressure release.
6. Discard the pandan leaf.

Simple Egg Spread

Serves: 4 | Cooking Time: 5 Minutes

Ingredients:

- 1 tbsp. olive oil
- 4 eggs
- 1 cup water
- Salt, to taste
- ½ cup mayonnaise
- 2 green onions, chopped

Directions:

1. Grease a baking dish with olive oil and crack the eggs in it.
2. Add the water and trivet to the Instant Pot. Place the baking dish on the trivet.
3. Lock the lid. Select the Manual mode, then set the timer for 5 minutes at High Pressure.
4. Once the timer goes off, do a natural pressure release for 3 to 5 minutes. Carefully open the lid.
5. Cool eggs down and mash them with a fork. Sprinkle with salt, mayo, and green onions. Stir well and serve immediately.

Cheesy Shrimp And Tomatoes

Serves: 6 | Cooking Time: 4 Minutes

Ingredients:

- 1 lb. shrimp, shelled and deveined
- 2 tbsps. butter
- 1 cup crumbled feta cheese
- 1½ cups chopped onion
- 15 oz. chopped canned tomatoes

Directions:

1. Set the Instant Pot to Sauté and melt the butter.
2. Add the onion, stir, and cook for 2 minutes.
3. Add the shrimp and tomatoes and mix well.
4. Lock the lid. Select the Manual mode, then set the timer for 2 minutes at Low Pressure.
5. Once the timer goes off, do a quick pressure release. Carefully open the lid.
6. Divide shrimp and tomatoes mixture into small bowls. Top with feta cheese and serve.

Coconut Pancake

Serves: 4 | Cooking Time: 40 Minutes

Ingredients:

- 1½ cups coconut milk
- 2 cups self-raising flour
- 2 eggs
- 1 tbsp. olive oil
- 2 tbsps. sugar

Directions:

1. In a bowl, mix eggs with sugar, milk and flour and whisk until you obtain a batter.
2. Grease the Instant Pot with oil, add the batter, spread into the pot.
3. Lock the lid. Set the Instant Pot to Manual mode, then set the timer for 40 minutes at Low Pressure.
4. When the timer goes off, perform a natural release for 10 minutes, then release any remaining pressure. Carefully open the lid.
5. Slice pancake, divide between plates and serve cold.

Sinfully Delicious Cinnamon Popcorn

Serves: 4 | Cooking Time: 10 Minutes

Ingredients:

- 2 tablespoons coconut oil
- 1/2 cup popcorn kernels
- 1/4 cup icing sugar
- 1/2 tablespoon ground cinnamon

Directions:

1. Press the "Sauté" button and melt the coconut oil. Stir until it begins to simmer.
2. Stir in the popcorn kernels and cover. When the popping slows down, press the "Cancel" button.
3. Toss the freshly popped corn with icing sugar and cinnamon. Toss to evenly coat the popcorn and serve immediately.

Vegan Coconut Mini Cheesecakes

Serves: 4 | Cooking Time: 45 Minutes

Ingredients:

- 1/2 cup almonds
- 1/2 cup sunflower kernels
- 6 dates, chopped
- 16 ounces coconut milk
- 3/4 cup coconut yogurt

Directions:

1. Spritz four ramekins with nonstick cooking spray.
2. Process the almonds, sunflower kernels, and dates in your blender until it turns into a sticky mixture.
3. Press the crust mixture into the prepared ramekins.
4. Thoroughly combine the coconut milk and yogurt in a mixing bowl. Pour this mixture into the ramekins and cover them with a piece of foil.
5. Place a metal trivet and 1 cup of water in your Instant Pot. Lower the ramekins onto the trivet.
6. Secure the lid. Choose the "Manual" mode and cook for 25 minutes at High pressure. Once cooking is complete, use a natural pressure release for 15 minutes; carefully remove the lid. Bon appétit!

Chocolate-strawberry Bars

Serves:6 | Cooking Time: 20 Minutes

Ingredients:

- ½ cup almond butter
- 2 cups strawberries
- 2 tbsp cocoa powder

Directions:

1. Place strawberries and almond butter in a bowl and mash with a fork. Add in cocoa powder and stir until well combined. Pour the strawberry and almond butter in a greased baking dish. Pour 1 cup of water in the pressure cooker and lower a trivet. Place the baking dish on top of the trivet and seal the lid. Select Manual and cook for 15 minutes at High. When it goes off, do a quick release. Let cool before cutting into squares.

Broccoli With Two-cheese And Chili Dip

Servings:6 | Cooking Time: 15 Minutes

Ingredients:

- 1 cup water
- 1 ½ pounds broccoli, broken into florets
- For the Sauce:
- 1 can of chili
- 1 cup Ricotta cheese, crumbled
- 1 ¼ cups Gruyère cheese shredded
- 1/4 cup salsa

Directions:

1. Add water to the base of your Instant Pot.
2. Put the broccoli florets into the steaming basket. Transfer the steaming basket to the Instant Pot.
3. Secure the lid. Choose the "Manual" mode and High pressure; cook for 3 minutes. Once cooking is complete, use a quick pressure release; carefully remove the lid.
4. Now, cook all sauce ingredients in a sauté pan that is preheated over medium-low flame. Cook for 7 minutes or until everything is incorporated.
5. Serve steamed broccoli with the sauce on the side. Bon appétit!

Lemon Mousse

Servings:6 | Cooking Time: 1 Hour

Ingredients:

- 3 or 4 large lemons
- ¾ cup sugar
- 4 tablespoons (½ stick) unsalted butter, at room temperature
- 4 large egg yolks
- Pinch kosher salt
- 1 cup heavy (whipping) cream

Directions:

1. Place the trivet in the inner pot, then pour in 1 cup water.
2. Zest 2 of the lemons. Set the zest aside, then halve the lemons and squeeze out 3 ounces of their juice. Set aside.
3. In a heatproof bowl, beat the sugar and butter with a hand mixer until the sugar has mostly dissolved and the mixture is light in color and fluffy. Add the egg yolks and beat until combined. Add the lemon zest,

lemon juice, and salt and beat to combine. The mixture will appear grainy; don't worry. Cover the bowl with aluminum foil, then place the bowl on the trivet.

4. Lock the lid into place. Select Pressure Cook or Manual; set the pressure to High and the time to 10 minutes.

5. After the cook time is complete, let the pressure release Naturally for 10 minutes, then Quick release any remaining pressure. Unlock and remove the lid. Let cool at room temperature for 20 minutes or so, then refrigerate, covered, until chilled, about 2 hours. Serve.

6. Carefully remove the bowl from the Instant Pot and remove the foil. The mixture will appear clumpy and curdled. Whisk the curd mixture until smooth. Place a fine strainer over a medium bowl and pour the curd through it, pressing down with a flexible spatula to pass the curd through, leaving the zest and any curdled egg bits behind. Be sure to scrape any curd on the bottom of the strainer into the bowl. Cover with plastic wrap, pushing the wrap down on top of the curd to keep a skin from forming. Refrigerate until set, 2 to 4 hours.

7. In a medium bowl, whip the cream with a hand mixer until medium-firm peaks form. Gently stir about one-third of the whipped cream into the curd until no streaks remain. Repeat with another third of the cream, folding it in gently, then fold in the last third. Serve immediately or cover and refrigerate up to overnight.

Ham And Cheese Dip

Serves: 4 | Cooking Time: 12 Minutes

Ingredients:

- 8 ham slices, chopped
- 2 tbsps. chopped parsley
- 8 oz. cream cheese
- 1 cup grated Cheddar cheese
- 1 cup Swiss cheese

Directions:

1. Set the Instant Pot to Sauté and brown the ham for 3 to 4 minutes.

2. Add the Swiss, Cheddar and cream cheese, and stir to combine well.

3. Lock the lid. Select the Manual mode, then set the timer for 6 minutes at High Pressure.

4. Once the timer goes off, do a natural pressure release for 5 minutes, then release any remaining pressure. Carefully open the lid.

5. Scatter the parsley all over and divide into bowls to serve.

Apple Cacao Dessert

Serves:2 | Cooking Time: 13 Minutes

Ingredients:

- 1 tbsp cinnamon
- 1 cup apples, chopped
- ½ cup milk
- 1 tbsp cacao powder
- 1 tbsp lemon juice

Directions:

1. Place apples, cinnamon, lemon juice, and ½ cup of water in your IP. Seal the lid, select Manual at High, and cook for 3 minutes. When done, do a quick pressure release. Mix in cacao powder, and blend well.

White Chocolate Fudge Sauce

Servings: 4 | Cooking Time: 15 Minutes

Ingredients:

- ¼ cup white chocolate, chopped
- 4 tbsp unsalted butter
- 2 cups heavy cream
- 3 tbsp granulated sugar
- 2 tbsp brandy

Directions:

1. In your Instant Pot, add heavy cream, sugar, butter, and white chocolate. Select Sauté and cook for 4 minutes.

2. After cooking, do a quick release, and unlock the lid. Whisk brandy into the mixture and pour into a serving jar. Serve.

Homemade Apricot Yogurt

Servings: 4 | Cooking Time: 8 Hours 20 Minutes + Cooling Time

Ingredients:

- 4 cups whole milk
- 2 packets yogurt starter
- 4 tsp apricot spread

Directions:

1. Set your Instant Pot to Sauté, pour in the milk, and bring to a boil. Remove to a heat-proof bowl and cool until a thermometer has reached a temperature of 110°F. Clean the inner pot.

2. In a bowl, pour 1 cup of cooled milk and mix in yogurt starter. Return to the pot and add in the remaining cooled milk; stir to combine. Seal the lid, select Yogurt, and cook for 8 hours. When done, do a quick pressure release. Unlock the lid and gently stir the yogurt. Divide the apricot spread between jars, top with yogurt, and let sit for 6 hours to thicken. Chill in the fridge and serve.

Simple Red Pepper Hummus

Serves: 4 | Cooking Time: 1 Hour 30 Minutes

Ingredients:

- ½ cup lemon juice
- 2 tbsps. sesame oil
- 1 tbsp. tahini paste
- 3 roasted red peppers
- 1 lb. chickpeas, soaked in water overnight

Directions:

1. In the Instant Pot, mix chickpeas with water.
2. Lock the lid. Select the Manual mode, then set the timer for 1 hour and 30 minutes at High Pressure.
3. Once the timer goes off, do a quick pressure release. Carefully open the lid.
4. Drain the chickpeas and transfer to a food processor. Add the roasted peppers, sesame oil, lemon juice, and tahini paste to the chickpeas, and pulse until it reaches your preferred consistency.
5. Serve immediately or refrigerate to chill until ready to use.

Balsamic Fennel With White Beans

Servings: 4 | Cooking Time: 40 Minutes

Ingredients:

- 2 tbsp olive oil
- 1 fennel bulb, thinly sliced
- 1 small red onion, chopped
- 1 cup dry white beans, soaked
- 3 cups vegetable broth
- 2 tbsp balsamic vinegar

Directions:

1. Set your Instant Pot to Sauté, heat olive oil, and sauté onion and fennel until softened, 3 minutes. Add white beans, broth, and balsamic vinegar. Seal the lid, select Bean/Chili, and set the cooking time to 30 minutes. After cooking, do a quick pressure release to let out steam and unlock the lid. Stir food, dish into serving plates, and serve warm.

APPENDIX : Recipes Index

Made in the USA
Middletown, DE
30 January 2023

23503246R00071